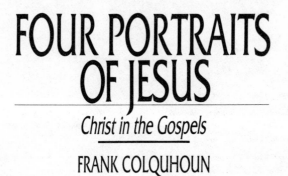

FOUR PORTRAITS
OF JESUS

Christic in the Gospels

FRANK COLQUHOUN

INTERVARSITY PRESS
DOWNERS GROVE, ILLINOIS 60515

© *Frank Colquhoun 1984*

*Published in the United States of America by InterVarsity Press, Downers Grove, Illinois,
with permission from A. R. Mowbray & Co. Ltd., Oxford, England. Originally titled*
Fourfold Portrait of Jesus.

*InterVarsity Press is the book-publishing division of Inter-Varsity Christian Fellowship, a
student movement active on campus at hundreds of universities, colleges and schools of
nursing. For information about local and regional activities, write IVCF, 233 Langdon St.,
Madison, WI 53703.*

*Distributed in Canada through InterVarsity Press, 860 Denison St., Unit 3, Markham,
Ontario L3R 4H1, Canada.*

Biblical quotations, unless stated otherwise, are from the Revised Standard Version.

Cover illustration: Diane Ameen-Newbern

ISBN 0-87784-450-X

Printed in the United States of America

Library of Congress Cataloging in Publication Data

Colquhoun, Frank.
  Four portraits of Jesus Christ in the Gospels.

  Originally published: Fourfold portrait of Jesus.
London: Mowbray, 1984.
    1. Bible. N.T. Gospels—Criticism, interpretation,
*etc.   2.   Jesus Christ—History of doctrines—Early
church, ca. 30-600.   I. Title.*
BS2555.2.C56   1985   226'.06   85-4248
ISBN 0-87784-450-X

16	15	14	13	12	11	10	9	8	7	6	5	4	3	2	1
98	97	96	95	94	93	92	91	90	89	88	87	86	85		

Preface

THE four Gospels are without dispute the most important books in the world for the Christian Church. In them we come face to face with the person of the historic Christ and learn from them nearly all that we know about him. It is therefore of prime importance that we should not only study them in piecemeal fashion, as we usually do, but also have a clear understanding of them as a whole.

My purpose in writing this short book is to help in that direction. It may be regarded as a simple, non-technical introduction to the Gospels for the ordinary Bible reader. It is not concerned with critical questions, though I have not ignored New Testament scholarship. I have gladly availed myself of it; but in these studies I have endeavoured as far as possible to let the Gospels speak for themselves, with a view to discerning the distinctive portrait of Christ they present to us and its relevance to our Christian faith and life.

I will only add that this is a book to be read alongside the Gospels, not instead of them. Those who study it in this way, with an open Bible at hand, are likely to get the most out of it and to encounter for themselves the Christ of the Gospels.

Prologue
The Four Records

IF we ask the question, What is Christianity? the shortest and simplest answer is, Christianity is Christ. As though in confirmation of that answer we find that, as soon as we open the New Testament, we are brought face to face with the person of Christ in the books we know as the four Gospels.

It is at those books we are going to look in broad outline, in order to discover what they tell us about Jesus Christ; and to begin with let us ask two questions. Why are these books called *Gospels*? And why are there *four* of them?

Properly speaking, the term 'Gospels' is a misnomer. As far as the New Testament is concerned there is only one Gospel: the good news of the saving acts of God accomplished in the life, death and resurrection of his Son Jesus Christ. In a true sense Christ himself *is* the Gospel. The words of Dr R. W. Dale remain valid, that Christ came not so much to preach the Gospel as that there might be a Gospel to be preached.

In the early centuries of the Church the whole collection of four books was given the one general title, *The Gospel*. The individual books were then differentiated by the addition of the words 'according to Matthew', 'according to Mark', and so on. The titles were intended to express the presentation of the one Gospel from the viewpoint of the four evangelists. In this way the essential unity of the books was recognized. However much they may differ from one another in content and style, the same good news about Jesus sounds out in all four.

But what is the point of having *four* records of our Lord's life and work? Would not a single account have been sufficient? Or if more than one was considered necessary, why limit the number to four?

It is an impressive fact that from an early date, well before the end of the second century, the four Gospels—they and none other—were accepted and recognized by the Church as part of the authentic Christian scriptures. Other so-called 'Gospels' were firmly rejected. So were attempts to turn the four into one composite volume. The Church was clear that all four records were needful; and we can understand why this should be so.

In the Gospels we are looking at the person of Jesus Christ through the eyes of four different writers; and these writers sought to portray him in distinctive ways, *in order to meet the particular needs of the people for whom they were writing*.

In the world to which Christ came there were three great historic races, each with its own features and its own significance in the life of the age.

There were the *Jews*, representing the religious element; for to the Jews God had revealed his law and given the promise of the coming of the Messiah.

There were the *Romans*, representing political power; for Rome was the undisputed master of that ancient world and by military might ruled over a far-flung empire.

There were the *Greeks*, representing the cultural and intellectual sphere; for while the Greeks were no

2

longer a political force, they dominated the world of literature and art, and the Greek language was spoken everywhere.

Into this world of the Jews, the Romans and the Greeks Christ came as the redeemer of mankind, and to its differing peoples his Gospel was preached in due course by his followers. As a result, out of these nations was formed a fourth nation, the 'holy nation' of the people of God (1 Peter 2.9)—that is, the *Church*.

Without being unduly fanciful it may be claimed that the four Gospels were written with these four different peoples in view:

> *Matthew* for the *Jews*, to demonstrate that Jesus of Nazareth was the promised Messiah of Israel;

> *Mark* for the *Romans*, to present Jesus as the anointed servant of the Lord in all his conquering power;

> *Luke* for the *Greeks*, to portray Jesus in the perfection of his humanity, the friend and saviour of all mankind;

> *John* for the *Church*, to reveal Jesus as the eternal Word made flesh, at once true God and true man.

Looked at in this light the Gospels provide a fourfold portrait of our Lord. Later we shall be taking a closer look at each portrait in turn so as to discern its distinctive features. Before we do so let us be clear about one or two matters.

The first thing to understand is that the Gospels are indeed *portraits*. They are not biographies. None of the evangelists set out to write a 'life' of Christ in the ordinary sense. Their accounts are too incomplete,

3

too fragmentary, to be regarded as that. What they provide is not a detailed story of what Jesus said and did but a portrait of him, designed to meet the requirements of their different readers.

The picture offered by each of the Gospels is a distinctive one, with its own clearly drawn features. That is why we need all four pictures and cannot afford to dispense with any of them. Every Gospel in turn adds something of value to our total understanding of the person of Christ and of the work he came to do for our salvation.

Again, while we recognize that the four portraits have their own characteristics, we must not exaggerate their differences or draw hard and fast lines between them. They all have much in common. They constantly supplement and complement each other. Each forms part of a whole. And it is only as we keep the whole portrait in view that we shall come to see the whole Christ.

1
Matthew
The Promised Messiah

The Gospel according to Matthew occupies pride of place in all the early lists of the books of the New Testament. It is in quite a special sense the *first* Gospel—and that for at least two good reasons.

To begin with, the primitive Church attached particular importance to this Gospel as offering the most complete and comprehensive account of the life and teaching of Jesus Christ. In those early centuries greater use was made of Matthew in the Church's worship, as well as in its preaching and teaching, than of any of the other Gospels.

In the second place, Matthew is essentially the *Jewish* Gospel: it sets the story of Jesus the Messiah against its Old Testament background. For this reason it may be regarded as the transitional Gospel, linking together the Old Testament and the New. Therefore in our Bibles it rightly comes immediately after the books that make up the Hebrew scriptures. By its very position it asserts that what God had promised of old he has fulfilled in the coming of Jesus.

That this is in essence the message of Matthew's Gospel is beyond dispute. You have only to turn to the very beginning of the Gospel to find the evidence. And here is a point worth noting: the opening of each Gospel provides a key to the understanding of that Gospel.

THE MESSIANIC KING

Note how Matthew's Gospel starts: 'The book of the genealogy of Jesus Christ, the son of David, the son of Abraham' (1.1). The person about whom this evangelist is writing is *Jesus Christ*—that is, Jesus the Messiah; and in this opening verse he is set before us in relation to two outstanding Old Testament figures.

(i) He is the son of *David*, the great king of Israel, and as such he is an heir of the royal house, destined to establish his kingdom among men and reign in righteousness.

(ii) He is the son of *Abraham*, the father of the Jewish nation, the one to whom God gave the promise that in his 'seed' all the families of the earth would be blessed (Genesis 12.3).

The genealogy that follows in verses 2–16 is not just a boring list of names. It has something important to say. In typical Jewish fashion the writer divides it into three sections of fourteen names each (see v. 17), the first section extending from Abraham to David (vv. 2–6a), the second from David to Jeconiah, the last of the kings of Israel (vv. 6b–11), and the third from the Babylonian captivity to the birth of Jesus (vv. 12–16). Note that each of the sections ends with the name of a king:

> The first section ends with David—the king who established the kingdom;
>
> the second section ends with Jeconiah—the king who lost the kingdom;
>
> the third section ends with 'Jesus who is called Christ'—the king who restored the kingdom.

Turn to the next chapter (ch. 2), the story of the magi or 'wise men' and their quest. It begins:

> Now when Jesus was born in Bethlehem of Judaea in the days of Herod the king, behold,

wise men from the east came to Jerusalem, saying, 'Where is he who has been born king of the Jews? For we have seen his star in the east, and have come to worship him.'

These men were seeking a king. Guided first by a star and later by the clearer light of scripture (vv. 5, 6) they came at length into the presence of the king— 'and they fell down and worshipped him. Then, opening their treasures, they offered him gifts, gold and frankincense and myrrh' (v. 11).

In striking pictorial form the story represents the gentile or heathen world seeking Jesus, bowing before him and presenting to him gifts worthy of a king. This is particularly significant in Matthew's Gospel, directed as it is to the Jewish people. The evangelist is reminding his readers at the outset that the Messiah has a world-wide mission to fulfil, as the prophets had foretold.

Note particularly one word in the story of the magi: 'they *worshipped* him'. The word is characteristic of this Gospel. Again and again we read of people coming to Jesus and offering him their worship.

For example, the man suffering from leprosy (8.2); the ruler of the synagogue at Capernaum (9.18); the disciples after the storm on the lake (14.33); the Canaanite woman (15.25); the mother of the sons of Zebedee (20.20); the disciples after the resurrection (28.9, 17). In each case the verb used (*proskuneo*) means to do obeisance, to render homage.

Son of David

Consider next the title *son of David*. As we have seen, it is the first title given to Jesus in Matthew's account (1.1). We meet with it again a number of times in later chapters. What does it signify?

Son of David is a royal title. Jesus is the man born to be king. The Jews of his day were looking for the coming of a king—the *Messiah*, as they called him. This is simply a Hebrew word which means the anointed one and which in Greek becomes *Christos*, Christ. The anointed king (or Messiah) for whom the Jews were looking would, they believed, be raised up in God's good time to rescue them from their foes (the Romans) and to establish his rule among them, in much the same way as David the illustrious warrior-king had conquered and reigned of old.

Clearly then 'son of David' was not only a messianic title. It was also a title with political and national overtones. This probably explains why Jesus himself was reluctant to be known as the son of David. It suggested the wrong sort of image. He was not the Messiah of popular expectation, the kind of king or saviour for whom the Jewish nation was waiting. He had come to save his people from their sins (1.21), not from their Roman overlords. This explains, too, why Jesus challenged the Jews about their whole concept of messiahship in terms of Son of David and lifted the title to far more spiritual level.

> While the Pharisees were gathered together, Jesus asked them a question, saying, 'What do you think of the Christ? Whose son is he?' They said to him, 'The son of David.' He said to them, 'How is it then that David, inspired by the Spirit, calls him Lord, saying,
>
> "The Lord said to my Lord,
> Sit at my right hand,
> till I put thy enemies under thy feet"?
>
> If David thus calls him Lord, how is he his son?' (22.41–45)

The words Jesus quoted to the Pharisees are from

Psalm 110.1. In the light of those words he insisted that the Christ or Messiah must be far more than the *son* of David. Under the inspiration of the Holy Spirit David himself calls the Messiah his *Lord*, not his son, and sees him exalted to the right hand of God, victorious over all his foes. So if the question is asked of the Messiah, 'Whose son is he?' it is not enough to say that he is the son of David and to think of him merely in terms of Jewish sovereignty and earthly power. He is also the Son of God whose throne is established in heaven and whose kingdom rules over all.

The Kingdom
But what is meant by the *kingdom*? Here is another key word which we need to understand. It occurs some eighty times in the Gospels; and while it is by no means peculiar to Matthew, it has a special significance in this Gospel, for a kingdom implies a king.

Matthew has his own distinctive way of designating the kingdom. Whereas the other Gospels speak about the kingdom of *God*, Matthew normally uses the expression 'the kingdom of *heaven*'. The reason is quite simple. Matthew is writing for Jews and 'kingdom of heaven' is a Jewish usage. Out of reverence for the divine name the Jews avoided wherever possible using the word 'God' and substituted some other term. Kingdom of heaven is the exact equivalent of kingdom of God and both mean the same—the rule or reign of God.

The kingdom of God is the kingship of God—the sovereignty of God operative in human life and society. This happens in effect wherever the claims of Christ are acknowledged and his teaching is put into practice. In a true sense the kingdom came with him,

9

came in a new and decisive way. Where Christ is, the kingdom is. But it is only imperfectly realized at present, which is why we continue to pray 'Thy kingdom come'. The consummation of the kingdom awaits the end of the age and the coming of the king to reign in power.

THE MESSIANIC PROMISE

No Jew would have had any interest in the story of one claiming to be the promised Christ unless he were convinced that the person in question fulfilled the messianic promises. So from beginning to end this Gospel is dominated by a constant reference to the Old Testament scriptures and by the writer's skilful use of those scriptures in relation to our Lord's life and work.

Turn again to the first chapter. After the genealogy the writer gives his account of how Jesus was born. Open your Bible and read verses 18–23. Do not let familiarity with the words blind you to their significance. Clearly Matthew tells the story of the nativity from the point of view of Joseph, just as Luke tells it from that of Mary. The accounts are therefore different, but they do not contradict. Both are agreed that Joseph, while being the lawful husband of Mary, was not the father of Jesus. They assert that Jesus was conceived in the womb of Mary by the operation of the Holy Spirit while she was still a virgin. Having related this, Matthew then adds (vv. 22, 23):

All this took place to fulfil what the Lord had spoken by the prophet:
'Behold, a virgin shall conceive and bear a son, and his name shall be called Emmanuel'
(which means, God with us).

10

The point of the prophecy quoted (Isaiah 7.14) is not so much to indicate the supernatural character of the Messiah's birth (that is, of the virgin) but to reveal its true *meaning*. Jesus is Emmanuel, *God* with us, God manifest in the flesh. The name bears witness at once to the mystery and the reality of the incarnation.

The second chapter of the Gospel contains further references to the Old Testament and its fulfilment in Jesus. When Herod the king inquired of the Jewish priests and scribes where the Messiah was to be born (vv. 3–6), they told him at once, 'In Bethlehem of Judaea; for so it is written by the prophet'—and they cited the well known words of Micah 5.2 about the little town of Bethlehem from which would emerge a ruler to govern God's people Israel.

Following the adoration of the magi we have the story of the flight into Egypt (vv. 13–15), where the holy family remained until the death of Herod. The writer says:

This was to fulfil what the Lord had spoken by the prophet, 'Out of Egypt have I called my son.' The words are from Hosea 11.1, where they refer to the deliverance of the Israelites from their Egyptian bondage in the time of Moses. Matthew applies the words to Jesus because he discerns a parallel between the history of Israel and the life of the Messiah. Jesus in fact is viewed as the *representative* Israelite who is one with his people, and the exodus is regarded as typifying *his* emergence from Egypt after the death of Herod.

Another reference to prophecy appears in what follows (vv. 16–18)—Herod's cruel and jealous slaughter of the young children of Bethlehem:

Then was fulfilled what was spoken by the prophet Jeremiah: 'A voice was heard in Ramah,

11

wailing and loud lamentation, Rachel weeping for her children; she refused to be consoled, because they were no more.'

In the passage quoted (Jer. 31.15) Rachel, the mother of Joseph and Benjamin, is described figuratively as weeping for her 'children' (her descendants) going into captivity in Babylon in Jeremiah's day. Her grief is seen by the evangelist to have its counterpart in the anguish of the bereaved mothers of Bethlehem.

Fulfilment

There are several other instances later in the Gospel where the writer quotes passages from the Old Testament to vindicate the claim that Jesus is the promised Messiah. 'That it might be fulfilled what was spoken by the prophet' is a phrase recurrent in Matthew.

For some further illustrations, see Matt. 4.12–16, where the fact that Jesus made Capernaum in Galilee the centre of his work is seen as foreshadowing his wider gentile mission, in accordance with Isaiah 9.1, 2; Matt. 8.16, 17, where his ministry of healing is declared to be in fulfilment of Isaiah 53.4; Matt. 13.35, where the Lord's parabolic method of teaching is said to accord with Psalm 78.2; and Matt. 27.9, where the use made by the priests of Judas's thirty pieces of silver (his 'blood money') is interpreted in reference to Zechariah 11.13.

Undoubtedly this argument from prophecy had a special appeal to Jewish readers, however arbitrary and artificial it may seem to us today. Its chief point was to make clear that Christ's earthly mission was no haphazard affair regulated by the designs of men, but the working out of a divine purpose and plan. Jesus himself was deeply conscious of this element in his life, and never more so than when he faced the final conflict of his passion. He met the treachery of Judas with the words, 'The Son of Man goes as it is written of him' (26.24); and in the garden of Gethsemane he declared, 'All this has taken place that the scriptures of the prophets might be fulfilled' (26.56).

By this appeal to prophecy Matthew's Gospel demonstrates the *continuity* of the New Testament with the Old. Christianity is not a completely new revelation. It is the consummation of Judaism. It is the fulfilment, the bringing to completion, of what had been promised.

The Church

These ideas are illustrated in Jesus' teaching about the *Church* in this Gospel—the only Gospel in which the word church (*ecclesia*) occurs. Hence Matthew is sometimes referred to as the ecclesiastical Gospel. It must be remembered that the Church, the people of God, is essentially an Old Testament concept. Jesus did not originate it: he developed it. And he did so in the first place by choosing *twelve* apostles as the nucleus of the new people of God (twelve was the number of the tribes of Israel).

There are three principal 'church sayings' of Jesus in the Gospel. The first and most significant is found in the words he spoke to Simon Peter after the apostle had confessed him to be the Messiah, the Son of God:

'Blessed are you, Simon Bar-Jonah! For flesh and blood has not revealed this to you, but my Father who is in heaven. And I tell you, you are Peter, and on this rock I will build my church, and the powers of death shall not prevail against it' (16.17, 18).

The word 'church' is used here in reference to the

13

universal Church; and Peter (*petros*) is designated as the rock (*petra*) on which this Church of the Messiah will be built. There are differing opinions about the interpretation of these words. What is clear beyond all question—and this is the really important thing—is that Christ himself is the *builder* of the Church, not Peter ('*I* will build'), and that likewise the Church *belongs* to Christ and not to any human being or institution ('*my* Church').

The next saying is about how a disciple of Jesus is to treat an offending brother who remains impenitent and refuses all attempts at reconciliation even in the presence of chosen witnesses. What is to be done then? Jesus says, 'if he refuses to listen to them, tell it to the church' (18.17). The 'church' here is the local congregation, which is authorized to exercise spiritual discipline among its members. In giving directions as to how the church is to act in such a case Jesus insists that there is no place for an impenitent sinner in the fellowship of his people. Those who have been forgiven must themselves be forgiving.

The third saying comes at the end of the Gospel, in the great commission of the risen Christ:

> 'All authority in heaven and on earth has been given to me. Go therefore and make disciples of all nations, baptizing them in the name of the Father and of the Son and of the Holy Spirit, teaching them to observe all that I have commanded you' (28.18–20).

The word 'church' does not actually occur here, but the Church is nevertheless depicted. It is seen now as a missionary body, acting under the Lord's divine authority and in obedience to his command—evangelizing the nations, baptizing new disciples, and teaching the faithful.

14

THE MESSIANIC TEACHING

One of the outstanding features of Matthew's Gospel is its record of the teaching of Jesus. That teaching is to be found throughout the Gospel, but most of it is gathered together in five great discourses in which the collected sayings of Jesus are arranged in a clear and orderly fashion.

The writer, as a Jew, had a particular liking for this sort of arrangement. It has a big advantage from a teaching point of view. The result is that in Matthew the messianic teaching is not so much chronological (in order of time) as topical (according to subject).

Open your Bible and look at the five discourses, each of which ends with the same general formula, 'When Jesus finished these sayings'. It has been suggested that the discourses were intended to be read within the Christian congregation and that the concluding formula means in effect, 'Here ends the first, second, third, fourth, fifth book of the oracles of Jesus the Messiah.'

The five discourses

(i) The first discourse is known to us as the sermon on the mount (chs. 5–7). Its general theme is *the ethics of the kingdom*. Beginning with the Beatitudes, it goes on to deal with the relation between the Mosaic law and the new righteousness of Christ (ch. 5); the three religious duties of almsgiving, prayer and fasting, and the necessity of daily trusting in God's fatherly care (ch. 6); and it concludes with various admonitions regarding true and false religion (ch. 7). Throughout Jesus stresses the quality of life and the standards of behaviour required of those who submit to God's sovereign rule.

(ii) The second discourse is the Lord's charge to the

twelve apostles as they set out on their missionary journey (ch. 10). The apostles are seen here as *the servants of the kingdom*; but clearly the teaching of Jesus in this chapter has been gathered from various sources and not all of it applies to the immediate mission of the twelve. It is designed to serve as a guide to the missionaries of the early Church—and indeed of all ages—as they face the task of proclaiming the good news of the kingdom in a hostile world.

(iii) The great parabolic discourse in chapter 13 is the third collection of our Lord's teaching. Seven parables are here brought together, four of which are peculiar to Matthew (the tares, the hidden treasure, the pearl of great price, and the drag-net). In general the parables illustrate *the progress of the kingdom*. From small and obscure beginnings, and despite all the activities of the enemy, the kingdom grows and prospers in the world, though its final triumph awaits what Jesus calls 'the close of the age' (39, 49).

(iv) In chapter 18 we have a collection of sayings concerned primarily with *the fellowship of the king-dom*. This discourse has been described as 'a little manual of instruction for the conduct of the organized Church'. As is clear from the quotation given in the previous section, it deals with such practical matters as personal relations, church discipline, and a forgiv-ing spirit. Aptly it concludes with the parable of the unmerciful servant.

(v) Last of all comes the striking discourse spoken on the Mount of Olives during passion week, dealing with the 'last things' and the coming (or *parousia*) of the Son of Man (chs. 24, 25). It points therefore to *the consummation of the kingdom*. The Lord surveys the course of the age through which his Church would have to pass and suffer and witness before his own return in glory. Much of the language is 'apocalyptic' or symbolical, expressed in vivid pictorial terms. The three parables of chapter 25 all illustrate in different ways the duty of *preparedness* for the coming of Christ and the final judgement.

Chief features
This is not the place to give a more detailed account of Christ's teaching in Matthew, but its chief features can be summed up as follows.

(i) The kingly authority of Jesus which underlies the teaching and challenges attention.
(ii) The sustained emphasis on the 'kingdom' or sovereign rule of God.
(iii) The strong moral note which runs through the teaching and relates it to life.
(iv) The interest in eschatology—that is, the last things, including the second coming and the judgement.
(v) The parabolic and pictorial form in which the teaching is presented.

THE MESSIANIC SIGNS

The remainder of the material in this Gospel is grouped around the five discourses at which we have been looking. Preceding them is the introduction to the story, extending from the birth of the Messiah to the beginning of the Galilean ministry (chs. 1–4); following them is the record of the Messiah's passion-victory (chs. 26–28); and inserted between them are various narrative sections.

From this the reader will get some idea of the way in which the evangelist has put together his material.

At the same time he will be able to make his own analysis of the contents of the Gospel.

In the narrative sections special attention is given to the *miracles* of Jesus. Here once again we have an example of Matthew's habit of grouping his material in an orderly way. Perhaps this is evidence that the writer had a methodical or even a mathematical mind. At any rate an examination of the Gospel as a whole reveals that he had a special fondness for threes and fives and sevens.

Take an example. In chapters 8 and 9, immediately following the sermon on the mount, no less than nine miracles are grouped together. In fact half of the miracles recorded in the Gospel are found in these two chapters. We can therefore be sure that the stories are not related in chronological order, as though the works were performed one after another. What the writer has done is to select nine typical miracles and arrange them in groups of three, to illustrate the differing ways in which Jesus exercised his messianic power and authority.

> The first group (8.1–15) consists of healing miracles and demonstrates Jesus' power over physical disease—leprosy, paralysis and fever.
> The second group (8.23–9.8) illustrates his supernatural authority in the realm of nature (stilling the storm), in the underworld of evil (exorcising the Gadarene demoniac), and in the moral sphere (forgiving sins).
> The third group (9.20–33) reveals him as the restorer of life, sight and speech.

The witness of the miracles
The miracles bear their own distinctive witness to the Lord's messianic mission. They were not simply

portents or 'stunts' designed to evoke wonder and astonishment. They were 'signs' that the New Age had dawned and that the Old Testament prophecies were being fulfilled. They were in a true sense the kingdom of God in action. They were vivid tokens that Jesus was indeed the person he claimed to be.

For example, look at the message of Jesus to John the Baptist, as recorded in chapter 11.2–6. From his gloomy dungeon John had sent his disciples to inquire of Jesus whether he really were the promised Messiah. 'Are you he who is to come, or shall we look for another?'

> Jesus answered them, 'Go and tell John what you hear and see: the blind receive their sight and the lame walk, lepers are cleansed and the deaf hear, and the dead are raised up, and the poor have good news preached to them. And blessed is he who takes no offence at me'.

The message was clear. The messianic signs testified to the messianic claims. John could be assured that Jesus was indeed the 'coming one' because the words of the prophet Isaiah were being enacted in the things that Jesus did (see, e.g. Isaiah 35.5; 61.1).

One other passage (which has already been quoted) must not be overlooked in this connection. The evangelist declares that Christ's work of exorcism and healing the sick was in fulfilment of Isaiah's words, 'He took our infirmities and bore our diseases' (8.16, 17). The words of the prophet (Isaiah 53.4) refer to the suffering servant with whom Jesus identified himself as the Messiah. In quoting them Matthew attaches an unusual meaning to the verbs *took* and *bore*, giving them the sense of carried away, removed, healed. The NEB rendering makes this clear: 'He took away our illnesses and lifted our diseases from us.'

THE MESSIANIC VICTORY

All four Gospels culminate in the crucifixion and resurrection of the Christ. To the early Church the death of Jesus and his rising again were so much of a piece that they could never be separated. And both were thought of in terms of *victory*. On the cross Jesus conquered the forces of evil arraigned against him, and his resurrection on the third day was the demonstration of that victory.

The king enters his city

In Matthew the passion story begins at chapter 21 with the triumphal entry into Jerusalem (vv. 1–11). That this was a messianic sign there can be no doubt. Jesus came to the holy city in a way that authenticated his claim to be the promised king, and it was as such that he offered himself to his people. But at the same time he made clear the kind of king he was. He came not as the conquering hero of popular expectations, but as a lowly king, riding upon an ass, a king of peace—in fulfilment of the prophecy in Zechariah 9.9, 10.

The cleansing of the temple (vv. 12, 13) was another messianic sign, an act of judgement upon a corrupt and degenerate religious system. By what he did Jesus virtually declared war on the Sadducees, the priestly party who had the monopoly of the temple and enriched themselves from its vast revenue. From this point onwards the battle was joined. The Sadducees and Pharisees alike were resolved to get Jesus out of the way. Humanly speaking, his fate was now sealed. But Jesus himself knew full well that the approaching sacrifice was not simply a matter of 'humanly speaking'. He was deeply conscious that the path he was treading was part of the divine purpose, and he moved forward to the cross with serene majesty. His kingliness is as evident in his passion as anywhere else in the Gospel. Take one or two illustrations.

Facing the cross
In the garden of Gethsemane Jesus, having bowed to the Father's will and accepted the 'cup' from his hands, meets the traitor's kiss and the blandishments of the armed rabble with imperial calm (26.47–54). He does not panic or resist. The hot-headed disciple who lashes out with his sword is at once reproved.

> Jesus said to him, 'Put your sword back into its place; for all who take the sword will perish by the sword. Do you think that I cannot appeal to my Father, and he will at once send me more than twelve legions of angels? But how then should the scriptures be fulfilled, that it must be so?'.

These verses, peculiar to Matthew, reveal the quiet dignity with which Jesus faced his assailants. He is in perfect command of himself and of the situation. He knows the way he must take. Having refused to be defended by the sword of man, he declines to be delivered by the angels of God. '*The scriptures must be fulfilled*'—this for him is the overriding consideration. And the scriptures declared that the Messiah must accomplish God's saving purpose, and pass to his ultimate glory, by suffering and death (cf. Luke 24.25–27).

Again, at his trial Jesus maintains a majestic silence before his accusers: 'he opened not his mouth' (Isaiah

21

53.7). The scene once more shows Jesus to be fully in control. He is not the helpless victim of circumstances. The prisoner is really the judge. It is the Jewish authorities who are on trial. As a last desperate resort the high priest puts Jesus on oath and asks him directly to inform the council whether he is the Messiah, the Son of God.

> Jesus said to him, 'You have said so. But I tell you, hereafter you will see the Son of Man seated at the right hand of Power, and coming on the clouds of heaven.' Then the high priest tore his robes, and said, 'He has uttered blasphemy. Why do we need further witnesses? You have now heard his blasphemy' (26.64, 65).

Using his own messianic title ('Son of Man') and echoing the words of Daniel 7.13 and Psalm 110.1, Jesus admits his identity. He *is* the promised king, and as such he is to be exalted to the throne of God and to reign in power and glory.

His words give the council what they are seeking. Without examining his claims they condemn Jesus as a false Messiah, and therefore guilty of blasphemy.

King for ever

So Jesus goes to the cross—a rejected king, his only crown a crown of thorns. Yet even in the final shame and agony of crucifixion his kingliness is apparent. The inscription over his head proclaims a profound truth: 'This is Jesus the King of the Jews'. He reigns even in death. The cross is his throne. And it may well be that the reference to the earthquake, the opened tombs, and the resurrection of departed saints at the moment Jesus died (27.51–53)—all peculiar to Matthew—is meant to convey to the reader the assurance that 'in the hour of his apparent defeat the regal power of the Messiah was being felt in the world of nature and in the realm of the departed' (R. V. G. Tasker, Tyndale Commentary, *Gospel according to St Matthew*, Inter-Varsity Press, 1971, pp. 25–26).

The resurrection as told in chapter 28 is the visible seal of the messianic victory. The story is dramatically related. Some have questioned the historicity of the strange and startling events in the opening verses. But at least there can be no doubt as to the symbolical value of those events. The violent earthquake and the descent of the shining angel, both alike striking terror into the hearts of the Roman guard, are to be understood as divine portents, indicating that *God* was at work in the happenings of that first Easter morning. The stone having been rolled back, the women are enabled to enter the tomb—only to find it empty. Jesus has already risen. The angel assures them of this fact and then gives them a special message: 'Go quickly and tell his disciples that he has risen from the dead, and behold, he is going before you to Galilee; there you will see him' (v. 7).

The allusion to Jesus going before his disciples to *Galilee* is particularly meaningful in this Gospel. 'Galilee of the gentiles', as it was known (see 4.15), signifies that Messiah's mission is to extend beyond Israel to the whole world.

So in the final verses—already quoted—the risen Christ claims total authority. All nations are to be evangelized. The universal Church is to be born, and the Lord's living presence will be with his people till the end of time. And his promise still remains: 'Lo, I am with you always, to the close of the age.'

2
Mark
The Anointed Servant

MARK'S Gospel is the shortest of the four. It is also by common consent the earliest; and its dynamic character makes it the easiest to read.

Early tradition unanimously connects the writing of it with a certain *person* and a certain *place*. The person is the apostle Peter and the place is Rome. Between them these two factors have a considerable bearing on the contents of the Gospel and go a long way to account for the distinctive picture of Jesus which emerges from its pages.

Christian writers from the second century onwards are agreed that John Mark was with Peter in Rome during the last part of the apostle's life and that he recorded in his Gospel the things that Peter preached about Jesus. Whether he wrote it before or after Peter's martyrdom (about the year 65) is not certain. What is certain is the close link between Mark's writing and Peter's preaching. The one is the record of the other.

This means that in putting together his story the evangelist was not drawing upon his own reminiscences or mere hearsay but upon first-hand and first-rate apostolic testimony. In fact in reading Mark's Gospel we are really seeing Jesus through the eyes of Simon Peter. The early Church recognized this, and one of the Church fathers actually quotes the Gospel under the title of 'the memoirs of Peter'.

Mark and Peter

The connection between the apostle and the evangelist does not depend solely on tradition. It has support in the New Testament itself. In 1 Peter 5.13 the apostle writes: 'She who is at Babylon, who is likewise chosen, sends you greetings, and so does my son Mark.' Here 'Babylon' is undoubtedly a pseudonym for Rome, and the 'she' is the Church in that city, from which Peter is writing this letter. With him at the time—the time of Nero's furious persecution of the Church in Rome—was Mark, whom Peter calls his 'son'. This is evidence that the two men were together in Rome and that there was a close spiritual bond between them. And if shortly afterwards, as is generally believed, Peter suffered martyrdom, it is not difficult to understand why Mark wrote his Gospel. The voice of the apostle was silenced, but his testimony must live on.

That Mark's Gospel is virtually Peter's Gospel is supported by a number of facts. One is that the story begins at the point where Peter's contact with Jesus began, with the ministry of John the Baptist (see John 1.35–42); and it ends with the special message of the angel to the women at the empty tomb, 'Go, tell his disciples *and Peter* that he is going before you to Galilee . . .' (16.7).

Again, the Gospel is full of vivid eye-witness touches. John Mark could not have been personally acquainted with the many details he records, for he himself was not an apostle. He must have obtained his information from one of the Lord's intimate companions who later recalled what he had seen. Who more likely to fulfil this role for Mark than Simon Peter?

Perhaps most significant of all is the picture of

Peter himself presented in this Gospel. He is scarcely ever mentioned except in derogatory terms. No attempt is made to disguise his blunders or excuse his failures. On the other hand scenes in which he played an honourable part tend to be passed over. Why is this? There seems only one explanation. Peter's own self-portrait, as it revealed itself in his preaching, is here faithfully recorded by his disciple John Mark.

One other point we ought to remember, and that is the connection of the Gospel not only with Peter but with *Rome*. Nearly all the historical evidence points to the fact that the evangelist wrote in the first instance with Roman readers in view. The internal evidence confirms this; for example, the writer's use of certain Latin words and the trouble he takes to explain Jewish customs. But most striking of all is the way in which Mark packs his story full of drama and movement and presents Jesus as a man of action.

The result is just the kind of picture that would have appealed to his readers. For the Romans were also men of action. They gloried in power and conquest; they were more interested in deeds than in words. Consequently the Christ of Mark's Gospel is one whom 'God anointed with the Holy Spirit and with power' and who 'went about doing good and healing all who were oppressed by the devil, for God was with him' (Peter's words, in Acts 10.38).

THE SERVANT'S ORDINATION

This concept of Jesus as the 'servant of the Lord' is basically Old Testament and goes back to the prophet Isaiah. It is an aspect of the *messiahship* of Jesus, but a very different one from that presented in the previous Gospel. *There* the Messiah is seen as the Davidic king, destined to be exalted to the right hand of God and to become the agent of God's kingly rule among men. In Mark the Messiah is identified with the suffering servant who accomplished his role as the redeemer of mankind by way of the cross (see Isaiah 53). But before he can enter upon his mission the Lord's servant must be commissioned and equipped for the task.

For the account of this we turn to the first chapter; and in doing so we are at once arrested by the opening words: 'The beginning of the gospel of Jesus Christ, the Son of God.' Mark makes clear that what he is about to relate is no ordinary story but *gospel* or good news, and that this good news finds its centre in no ordinary person but in the *Son of God*. He wants to impress upon his readers at the outset that the one of whom he is writing is a divine person, supernatural in origin and therefore supernatural in power.

The baptism
There follows a brief account of the ministry of John the Baptist, leading directly to the baptism of Jesus:

> In those days Jesus came from Nazareth in Galilee and was baptized by John in the Jordan. And when he came up out of the water, immediately he saw the heavens opened and the Spirit descending upon him like a dove; and a voice came from heaven, 'Thou art my beloved Son; with thee I am well pleased' (1.9–11).

The baptism of Jesus has been called 'the ordination of the Servant Messiah'. Why? Because of the *voice* and the *vision*. The heavenly voice acknowledged Jesus to be the Father's beloved Son, while the words 'with thee I am well pleased' designated him as the Lord's chosen servant, endued with the Spirit, in accordance with the well known prophecy of Isaiah

42.1 (look this up). And so the voice was accompanied by the vision: the descent of the Spirit in the form of a dove. This represented the servant's anointing with power for the ministry he was called to fulfil, both by his life and by his death.

Clearly the story is told in symbolical language; but equally clearly the language is pregnant with meaning. On the very first page of Mark's Gospel we are confronted with one who, though truly Son of God in a unique sense, is also truly man, the anointed servant whose destiny is to redeem mankind by treading the path of suffering.

The story of the baptism is followed by a short account of the temptation in the wilderness. For all its brevity it is remarkably graphic:

> The Spirit immediately drove him out into the wilderness. And he was in the wilderness forty days, tempted by Satan; and he was with the wild beasts; and the angels ministered to him (1.12, 13).

The temptation marks the testing of the servant for his future ministry. It also indicates the conditions under which the ministry is to be fulfilled. Throughout his life of service Jesus is to be led by the Spirit, opposed by Satan, attended by angels, and to show himself the Lord of creation.

THE SERVANT IN ACTION
The Lord's servant, tested and triumphant, is now ready to embark upon his public work. The story of this begins at verse 14 of the first chapter. Note carefully that fact. After only a dozen or so verses we have reached a point in Mark's Gospel which Matthew and Luke arrive at three chapters later. It seems that Mark has no time for the preliminaries. He

dismisses them as briefly as possible. He is impatient to get to the heart of the matter and to show the Servant in action. So he plunges straight into his subject.

Following the arrest of John the Baptist Jesus comes from Judaea into Galilee, preaching the good news about God, announcing the advent of the kingdom, and calling people to repentance and faith. As he walks along the shore of the Sea of Galilee he sees some fishermen at work. From among these hardy working-class Galileans he recruits his first disciples. To four of them, two pairs of brothers, he issues his call—'Follow me!' The result was instantaneous: 'Immediately they left their nets and followed him.'

'*Immediately*'. That is one of Mark's favourite words. It occurs forty-one times in his Gospel, and no less than ten times in this first chapter (vv. 10, 12, 18, 20, 21, 23, 28, 29, 30, 42). The word imparts to the story a certain urgency, a sense of movement, an air of breathless activity. Wherever Jesus goes things are happening—and happening with the least possible delay.

What next? Read on in the first chapter and you find a vivid account of a wonderful sabbath at Capernaum (vv. 21–34). Jesus is teaching in the synagogue, and the authority of his teaching creates a profound impression on the hearers. But all at once ('immediately') he is rudely interrupted. A man in the congregation possessed with an unclean spirit cries out, 'What have you to do with us, Jesus of Nazareth? Have you come to destroy us? I know who you are, the Holy One of God.' With the same authority that marked his teaching Jesus rebuked the unclean spirit and cast it out.

Exorcism

This is Mark's first recorded miracle of Jesus. Significantly it is a miracle of exorcism, for the evangelist shows a particular interest in this type of healing. Two further references to casting out of demons occur later in this same chapter (vv. 32–34, 39). Doubtless Mark saw in these works of exorcism a striking demonstration of the Lord's supreme power in the spiritual realm, his mastery of the underworld of evil. This is the real significance of the exorcisms referred to in this Gospel (see 3.11, 22 ff.; 5.1–20; 6.7, 13; 7.25 ff.; 9.14 ff.).

Admittedly to modern minds the whole question of demon possession presents a bigger problem than it did to the people of Jesus' day. But however glibly we may dismiss evil spirits as belonging to the thought-forms of a past age, we cannot so easily explain away the fact of evil itself as a grim reality in today's world. Not all that is wrong with human personality can be accounted for in psychological terms or cured by medical means. In so far as evil is a spiritual force it can only be conquered by spiritual means.

Mark continues his narrative of the sabbath at Capernaum by relating how Jesus, on returning from the synagogue, cured Peter's mother-in-law of her fever and of how at sunset, when the sabbath was technically over, he healed many who were sick and cast out many demons (vv. 29–34). It was the end of a day of almost incessant activity. Nevertheless, early the next morning, 'a great while before day', he left the house and went out to a lonely place to pray. It was there that the disciples later found him in communion with his Father (vv. 35–39).

The incident is a revealing one. The power that went forth from Jesus was not some form of magic. It was power derived from God, exercised by one who was in unbroken fellowship with God and perfectly in line with his will. It is this fact that must be remembered in reading the miracle stories in the Gospels. The key to the things that Jesus did lies in the person that Jesus was. It is pointless to object to the stories on the score that we ourselves have never seen such things happen. That is true. But then we have never seen a man like Jesus confronted by human suffering and the power of evil. The miracles, as Professor C. F. D. Moule remarks, 'always seem to have been the result, simply, of Jesus's concern for people and his perfect and absolute obedience, as Son of God, to the will of his Father' (*Cambridge Bible Commentary, St Mark*, CUP, 1965, p. 15).

The subject is important as we look at Mark's portrait of Jesus because of the prominent place that miracles occupy in the Gospel. Approximately one third of the whole book is taken up with the 'mighty works'. Unlike Matthew, Mark does not record much of the teaching of Jesus. For example, he gives only four of the parables, one of which is peculiar to his Gospel (4.26–29). On the other hand there are no less than eighteen miracles in Mark, apart from a number of general statements about the Lord's healing ministry.

The compassionate Christ

Clearly then the Christ of this Gospel is the conquering Christ, exercising his power over demons, disease and death. But that is not all. He is also the *compassionate* Christ, wonderfully human, gracious, sympathetic and understanding. Without this touch Mark's portrait would lose much of its appeal. Power divorced from love is not an attractive quality.

31

Let us look at a few examples.

Jesus is moved with pity for the leper who comes to him for cleansing (1.41).

He looks with anger on those who would have dissuaded him from healing the man with the withered hand (3.5).

He has compassion on the crowds that throng him when he is seeking rest (6.34).

He is indignant with his disciples when they try to prevent the children being brought to him, and tenderly takes the little ones into his arms (10.13–16).

He looks with real affection on the rich young ruler who comes to him seeking eternal life (10.21).

Such is the anointed servant of Mark's Gospel. The Spirit of power that rests upon him is also the Spirit of love. The warm human compassion of Jesus shines forth again and again as he pursues his ministry and goes about doing good, healing the sick and helping the needy—a man who is able to sympathize with our weaknesses (Heb. 4.15).

THE SUFFERING SERVANT

A key verse of this Gospel is doubtless the one which records the words of Jesus when, in teaching his disciples to put *service* before self, he pointed to his own example:

The Son of Man came not to be served, but to serve, and to give his life as a ransom for many (10.45).

The whole of Jesus' life was one of service. That is why Mark portrays him as the Lord's servant. But he is the *suffering* servant: the one who at the last crowns his service with his sacrifice. This is the total picture of the Lord in Mark's Gospel. Over the first half of the record could be inscribed the words, 'The Son of Man came to serve'; over the second half, 'The Son of Man came to give his life as a ransom for many.'

The turning point

The dividing point in the story comes in the middle of the Gospel at chapter 8. Jesus has taken his disciples apart to the far north of the country, in the neighbourhood of Caesarea Philippi. He wants to have them alone with himself in order to prepare them for the final and decisive phase of his ministry. He has a revelation to make to them; but first he questions them.

'Who do men say that I am?' he asks. They tell him the popular opinion. Men think of him in terms of John the Baptist or one of the great prophets of old. As a man he is seen to be someone out of the ordinary; a remarkable man, no doubt, but no more than that.

'But *you*—who do you say that I am?' The question now becomes personal; and Peter makes his great confession: 'You are the Christ!' It was a tremendous affirmation, the biggest thing a Jew could say of anyone. Slowly but surely the conviction had grown among the twelve that Jesus was no mere man, not even a heaven-sent prophet like the Baptist, but none other than the long awaited Messiah.

Jesus accepted Peter's testimony, but at the same time he shattered the disciples' dreams. He was indeed the Messiah but not the kind of Messiah they were expecting.

> He began to teach them that the Son of Man must suffer many things, and be rejected by the elders and the chief priests and the scribes, and be killed, and after three days rise again. And he

said this plainly. And Peter took him, and began to rebuke him. But turning and seeing his disciples, he rebuked Peter, and said, 'Get behind me, Satan! For you are not on the side of God, but of men' (8.31–33).

Poor Peter! Here was something he simply could not understand—'the Son of Man *must suffer* . . .'. It was an entirely new concept of messiahship. Yet Jesus was insistent that this was his destined role. In his mind, quite clearly, was the picture of the suffering servant of Isaiah 53. He was going to Jerusalem not to be crowned but to be crucified. In his bewilderment Peter felt obliged to protest—only to meet with the Lord's sharp rebuke, 'Get behind me, Satan!' Unconsciously the apostle was echoing the voice of the devil in the wilderness, tempting Jesus to follow the easy way and by-pass the cross (cf. Matt. 4.10).

This revelation of the passion had doubtless left the disciples incredulous and mystified; and that is why a few days later the transfiguration took place (9.2–8). Its purpose was to confirm the faith of the disciples and to vindicate the person of Christ. In that transcendental moment on the mountain top the three disciples (including Peter) caught a glimpse of his divine glory as the messianic king and heard the voice of the Father acclaiming him as his beloved Son; while the appearance of the two Old Testament saints talking with Jesus signified that his chosen path of suffering was in accordance with the scriptures, the testimony of the law and the prophets.

The way of the cross
From this point onwards the cross is the dominant theme of the Gospel. As he came down the mountain with the disciples the Lord reverted to the subject. He

charged them to tell no one what they had seen 'until the Son of Man should have risen from the dead' and asserted that it was 'written of the Son of Man that he should suffer many things and be treated with contempt' (9.9–13). All the time Jesus was preparing his followers for what was to befall him in Jerusalem.

Two other predictions of the passion come soon after. The first follows the healing of the epileptic boy at the foot of the mountain.

> They went on from there and passed through Galilee. And he would not have anyone know it; for he was teaching his disciples, saying to them, 'The Son of Man will be delivered into the hands of men, and they will kill him; and when he is killed, after three days he will rise.' But they did not understand the saying, and they were afraid to ask him (9.30–32).

A little later we are given a deeply impressive picture of Jesus: a lonely figure striding on ahead along the road to Jerusalem, while his disciples hang back, overawed by the fortitude and resolution of their master as he goes forward to his death. That this is indeed the subject of his thoughts is revealed in his third prediction of the passion:

> Taking the twelve again, he began to tell them what was to happen to him, saying, 'Behold, we are going up to Jerusalem; and the Son of Man will be delivered to the chief priests and the scribes, and they will condemn him to death, and deliver him to the Gentiles; and they will mock him, and spit upon him, and scourge him, and kill him; and after three days he will rise' (10.32–34).

Before we reach the end of this tenth chapter Jesus has arrived at Jericho; and the beginning of the next chapter tells the story of his triumphal entry into the holy city. In spite of the shouts of the crowd proclaiming him king, he knows that the welcome accorded him will be short lived, He is not the sort of king the people are looking for. He is riding to the throne which his Father has appointed for him—and that throne is a cross.

The suffering Church

The picture of the suffering Christ in this Gospel would have had special significance for its first readers. For the Church in Rome at the time Mark wrote his story was a suffering Church, undergoing bitter persecution under the infamous emperor Nero. It was during that persecution, as we have already noted, that the apostle Peter was put to death—and almost certainly St Paul as well. In view of this situation it is more than probable that one of the reasons why Mark placed so much emphasis on the passion was to encourage the believers in Rome to endure their afflictions bravely and to remind them that they were treading in the steps of their Lord.

One of the features of this Gospel is the hostility Jesus met with from the religious leaders of the day. The opposition becomes apparent at a very early stage. After Jesus had healed the man with a withered arm on the sabbath we are told that the Pharisees 'immediately held counsel with the Herodians against him, how to destroy him' (3.6). It was an unholy alliance. In the ordinary way the Pharisees and Herodians would never have dreamed of conspiring together, for they were deeply divided; but now they readily joined forces in their common determination to get Jesus out of the way.

From this point onwards he is continually facing

rejection, persecution—and finally death. It is noteworthy that immediately after Peter's great confession of him as the Messiah he not only insisted that messiahship for *him* meant suffering. He likewise insisted that those who choose to follow him must be prepared to share his suffering: 'If any man would come after me, let him deny himself and take up his cross and follow me' (8.31–34). The way of the cross is the appointed way for the disciple as well as for the master—the cross of suffering, sacrifice and shame.

It is of this uncomfortable truth that Mark is reminding the suffering Church in Rome in the passion narratives. And the truth is one for the Church of all time, not least for the Church of our own day. To suffer for Christ is to suffer with Christ. It is part of the cost of discipleship. But that is not all. Jesus triumphed in his suffering. He conquered death. The cross was followed by the glory of the resurrection. And this too is the pattern of Christian discipleship. Those who suffer with him will also be glorified with him (Romans 8.17; 2 Timothy 2.12).

THE SERVANT OBEDIENT UNTO DEATH

In his great hymn of the incarnation (Philippians 2.5–11) St Paul says that the Son of God in becoming man 'took the form of a servant', and that having thus humbled himself he 'became obedient unto death, even death on a cross'. In his record of the passion Mark tells us how this happened.

The story of the last great week in Jerusalem—from what we know as Palm Sunday to Easter Day—occupies approximately one third of the entire Gospel (chapters 11–16). The story is related in considerable detail, and at this point the narrative takes on a new coherence. It is almost as though all that had happened before was an introduction to the story proper, in order to explain how the death of Jesus came about. This quite literally is the crux of the Gospel.

The last week

The events of that last week are related with stark realism and many graphic touches, typical of this Gospel. But for the reader there is something that matters more than the events themselves. The question is, what do they *mean*? How are we to interpret the passion? Why did Jesus die?

Mark provides some clues by way of answer. In his passion narrative he not only sets forth Jesus as the suffering servant; at the same time he makes clear the vicarious nature of his sufferings. In fulfilment of Isaiah's prophecy Jesus becomes obedient to the death on the cross *for the sake of others*. He, the sinless one, 'bore the sin of many' (Isaiah 53.12). In a word, his death is not simply an example: it is a work of atonement. By means of that death sin is dealt with, a new covenant is established, and the kingdom of heaven is opened to all believers.

Take two passages by way of illustration. The first describes what happened in the upper room when Jesus gathered with his disciples for the last supper.

> As they were eating, he took bread, and blessed, and broke it, and gave it to them, and said, 'Take; this is my body.' And he took a cup, and when he had given thanks he gave it to them, and they all drank of it. And he said to them, 'This is my blood of the covenant, which is poured out for many.'

It was passover time. The occasion therefore had a sacrificial background. It was through the blood of the passover lamb that redemption came to the enslaved Israelites in Egypt (Exodus 12.1–13). Later, under the shadow of Mount Sinai, Moses took the blood of sacrifice and with it inaugurated a solemn covenant between God and his redeemed people (Exodus 24.3–8).

Only against this background can we understand the significance of the meal over which the Lord presided on that dark night in which he was betrayed. The broken bread and outpoured wine were the tokens of the coming sacrifice by which he was to accomplish a greater redemption than that of the passover. And by that sacrifice he was to establish a new covenant and bring mankind into a new relationship with God, as Jeremiah had foretold (31.31–34). And all this because his blood was to be 'poured out for many'—again a phrase reminiscent of the servant song of Isaiah 53 (v. 12).

The crucifixion
We turn next to Mark's account of the crucifixion (15.21–39). Once more the picture is one of vicarious suffering. Even the mockery of the high priests unconsciously reflected the truth: 'He saved others; he cannot save himself' (v. 31). They were wrong in one respect, of course. Jesus *could* have saved himself, if he had chosen. But they were right in this: he could not save himself *and* save others. To save others he must sacrifice himself. This was why he went to the cross. He was the man for others in his death as in his life.

Mark records only one of the Lord's words from the cross, the terrible cry of spiritual dereliction, 'My God, my God, why hast thou forsaken me?' It is impossible to understand such words except in terms of sin-bearing love. On the cross Jesus identified himself with our sin, accepted responsibility for it, and suffered its consequence—separation from God. The Lord laid on him the iniquity of us all (Isaiah 53.6; cf. 2 Corinthians 5.19–21).

Note next the rending of the temple 'veil', the heavy curtain which separated the holy place from the holy of holies, forbidding access to God's presence. But now the curtain is ripped in two, as though by a divine hand, 'from top to bottom' (v. 38). The symbolism is unmistakable. Because of the death of Jesus the way to God is open to sinful men, a 'new and living way', as the writer to the Hebrews expresses it (10.19–22).

But not only is the way to God open: it is open to *all*, Jew and gentile alike. The Roman centurion, witnessing the final scenes and arrested by the way Jesus died, exclaims, 'Truly this man was a son of God!' (v. 39). It is not certain how much we ought to read into his words, but one thing at least is clear. This pagan soldier at the cross represents the gentile world confessing the faith of Christ crucified.

The empty tomb
But Mark's story does not end with a crucified Christ, a dead Jesus. Had it done so it would have been no 'gospel', and indeed the story would never have been written. The record of the passion is itself evidence for the resurrection, since it could never have been included as part of the good news except by those who believed in the risen Lord.

Mark's account of the resurrection is brief but vivid (16.1–8). He portrays the women hastening to the tomb in the early morning to embalm the body of Jesus—only to find that they are too late. The tomb is empty. The body is not there. And they are met with the astonishing news, 'You seek Jesus of Nazareth who was crucified. He has risen, he is not here.'

'*He has risen*'—risen as he himself repeatedly declared would happen. In foretelling his passion Jesus had at the same time foretold his resurrection on the third day. And this, let us note, was in accordance with the destined role of the Lord's servant in Isaiah. The servant suffers; but the servant also triumphs. 'Behold, my servant shall prosper, he shall be exalted and lifted up, and shall be very high (Isaiah 52.13).

As the reader probably knows, and as all modern translations make clear, the authentic text of Mark's Gospel breaks off abruptly at verse 8 of chapter 16. The remaining verses (9–20) are not in the oldest and best Greek manuscripts and were clearly added later by some other hand to round off the story. The evangelist's original ending must have been lost or destroyed at an early date.

But while the Gospel as Mark wrote it is thus incomplete, it is certainly not inconclusive. The mighty works of Christ, which are such an outstanding feature of this book, are now crowned by the mightiest miracle of all—the resurrection. That much is clear, despite the lost ending. The tomb is empty. Christ is alive. Death is vanquished. And this is 'gospel'—good news for all mankind, and good news for us still today.

3
Luke
The Universal Saviour

LUKE was a gentile, a Greek by race. He has the distinction of being the only non-Jew among the writers of the New Testament. He also has the distinction of having written more of the New Testament than any other person. His two books—the Gospel which bears his name and its sequel, the Acts of the Apostles—make up nearly a quarter of the entire volume. Clearly our indebtedness to Luke is incalculable. Without his writings our knowledge of Jesus and the early Church would be very much the poorer.

It is St Paul who in Colossians 4.11–14 tells us that Luke was a gentile (he names him among his non-Jewish companions) and that by profession he was a doctor—'the beloved physician'. He was the apostle's close friend and travelling companion, who shared his imprisonment at Rome and was with him faithfully to the end (2 Tim.4.11). His Gospel shows how much he had absorbed of Paul's evangelical teaching and outlook.

The preface
The book begins with a formal introduction and dedication (1.1–4). Here again, as in the other

Gospels, the opening words are significant and provide a clue to the book and the writer's intentions.

Inasmuch as many have undertaken to compile a narrative of the things which have been accomplished among us, just as they were delivered to us by those who from the beginning were eye-witnesses and ministers of the word, it seemed good to me also, having followed all things closely for some time past, to write an orderly account for you, most excellent Theophilus, that you may know the truth concerning the things of which you have been informed.

(i) This preface tells us something about the *writer*. It reveals Luke as a highly educated and scholarly man, for it is written in polished classical Greek, not the common Greek spoken at that time.

(ii) It tells us something about his *sources*. He had derived his information both from written documents and from the testimony of eye-witnesses.

(iii) It tells us something about his *method*. He had carefully investigated the historical facts and 'gone over the whole course of these events in detail', in order to produce 'a connected narrative' (NEB).

(iv) Finally, it tells us something about his *aim*, which was to establish the truth and credibility of the Christian faith.

The Gospel is dedicated to Theophilus (a Greek name meaning 'lover of God'), who may be regarded as a representative of the cultured Greek world of that day. So Luke, himself a Greek, writes especially for the Greeks, as early tradition asserts. His vocabulary and style of writing confirm the fact. His is the most literary of the Gospels. In its Greekness and in its elegance and beauty Luke's work is, as Dr William

Barclay asserts, 'an attempt to present Christianity to a new audience without at the same time forgetting the ordinary people.'

The Greeks were not only deeply interested in beauty, art and literature. They also cherished high ideals of humanity and prided themselves on their broad sympathies, their worldwide outlook. Luke therefore sets before his readers a marvellous portrait of Jesus as the saviour of all mankind, emphasizing continually the perfection of his manhood and the universal range of his saving mission.

Scholars are agreed that *salvation* provides the clue to the theology of Luke. It is also the key to his portrait of the Lord, as we shall see. But first we must go back to the beginning of the story.

THE SAVIOUR PROMISED LONG

At first sight Luke's Gospel seems to start in rather a strange way, considering that it was written primarily for gentile readers. It begins in the temple at Jerusalem, and the first two chapters have a strongly Jewish flavour. The idiom is Hebrew rather than Greek; the whole atmosphere is reminiscent of the Old Testament.

But there is a good reason for this. As an historian Luke is tracing the Christian story back to its origins, and in doing so he makes clear that *Christianity was cradled in Judaism*. The coming of Jesus was not something out of the blue, so to speak, disconnected with the past. It was in all its aspects 'according to the scriptures' (cf. 1 Cor. 15.3–4). So at the outset the evangelist is saying to us, in the words of the Advent hymn,

'Hark the glad sound! the Saviour comes,
The Saviour promised long!

The story therefore begins on the note of fulfilment. The birth of Jesus and all that followed from it is seen to be the unfolding of a divine purpose and plan.

Visions and prophecies

All this is made plain in these two opening chapters. They are the record of a series of visions and prophecies, all of which point to Jesus as the long-promised Saviour.

Note carefully the three visions of angels—or perhaps we should call them angelic visitations. The first of these was granted to Zechariah as he ministered in the temple (1.8–17). The angel announced to the incredulous priest that his aged wife Elizabeth was to bear a child, to be named John, who would be the forerunner of the Messiah, the one sent to prepare the way of his coming.

But how and when was the Messiah to come? The answer is given in the second vision (1.26–38) when the same angel appeared to Mary of Nazareth and told her she had found favour with God:

'For behold, you will conceive in your womb and bear a son, and you shall call his name Jesus. He will be great, and will be called the Son of the Most High; and the Lord God will give to him the throne of his father David, and he will reign over the house of Jacob for ever; and of his kingdom there will be no end.'

The third vision was seen by the shepherds of Bethlehem keeping watch over their flock by night (2.8–14). In the previous visitations the Messiah's birth had been *foretold*. Now the good news is announced that the event has taken place: 'for to you is born this day in the city of David a Saviour, who is Christ (Messiah) the Lord.'

The prophecies that accompany the visions are equally important. We must remember that for centuries the voice of prophecy had been silent in Israel. Now, with the advent of the Messiah, it sounds out again. It is heard in the sacred songs which characterize these early chapters: in the *Magnificat* of Mary (1.46–55), the *Benedictus* of Zechariah (1.67–79), and the *Nunc Dimittis* of Simeon (2.29–32). Both Mary and Zechariah acknowledge God's faithfulness in fulfilling his promise to the Jewish nation, a promise going back to the time of Abraham and confirmed by the prophets of a later age. And the old man Simeon declares that the infant Jesus whom he holds in his arms is destined to be not only the glory of Israel but God's salvation for all the nations.

Throughout the infancy narratives Luke is making clear that something very wonderful, something supernatural, is happening. The coming of Jesus Christ into the world is the great turning point of history, and through that event God is working out his purpose for the redemption of mankind.

THE SAVIOUR OF THE WORLD

The Gospel story, though it was all enacted in the small and seemingly insignificant country of Palestine (no bigger than Wales), is in fact the record of a world event. Luke indicates this by setting it in the context of Roman history (see 2.1 and 3.1 where he names the Caesars or emperors who ruled at the time). So from the Hebrew background at which we have been looking Jesus emerges as a cosmic figure. He is indeed the promised Messiah of Israel, but he is more than that. He is also the bringer of salvation to the gentiles, as Simeon had foretold.

One of the clearest and strongest notes in Luke's

Gospel is that of *universalism*. Christ is the redeemer of all mankind. There are numerous instances of this.

(i) It is Luke alone of the evangelists who, having applied the prophecy of Isaiah 40.3–5 to John the Baptist as 'the voice of one crying in the wilderness', completes the quotation with the words 'and *all flesh* shall see the salvation of God'.

(ii) In Luke the genealogy of Jesus is traced back to *Adam*, the father of the human race (3.23–38)—not as in Matthew to Abraham, the father of the Jewish nation.

(iii) Luke tells us how, at the beginning of his ministry, Jesus preached on the sabbath in the synagogue at Nazareth and incurred the wrath of his own townsfolk by recalling that the prophets Elijah and Elisha ministered not only to Israelites but also to heathen people such as a Sidonian widow and a Syrian soldier (4.24–28). Jesus was indicating that his salvation was for others than the Jews.

The Samaritans

(iv) Luke draws attention to the Lord's special interest in Samaritans—people whom the Jews regarded as aliens and outsiders. The Samaritans were the descendants of Israelites who during the Exile had intermarried with the heathen Assyrians in the land. They were thus people of mixed race, and worse still of mixed religion; for they accepted only the books of Moses as scripture and worshipped in their own temple which they had built on Mount Gerizim. The Jews refused to have any dealings with them.

But Jesus adopted an entirely different attitude towards them. He rebuked his disciples when they wanted to call down fire from heaven on some Samaritan villagers who had refused him hospitality

(9.51–56). On the other hand, in one of his best known parables, he held up a Samaritan as a shining example of true neighbourliness (10.30–37). And again, after the cleansing of the ten lepers who had cried to him for mercy, he had a special word of commendation for the only one among them who returned to give thanks—'and he was a Samaritan' (17.11–19).

These examples are sufficient to illustrate the cosmopolitan character of Luke's Gospel. The Jesus he portrays is the Saviour of the world, the whole world, irrespective of race or nationality. Again and again, by his record of what Jesus said and did, the evangelist affirms the truth of St Paul's words, 'There is neither Jew nor Greek, . . . for you are all one in Christ Jesus' (Gal. 3.28). At the time of Jesus's ministry this was a revolutionary truth. Its full implications were not grasped by the Church until later, and then only slowly, as Luke reveals in the Acts.

But the truth was implicit from the beginning in what Jesus himself did and taught, as this Gospel makes plain. He totally rejected any idea of racial discrimination. To him all people were of equal worth and his saving work on the cross embraced them all. So all must hear the good news; hence his final words to his disciples at the end of the story:

'Thus it is written, that the Christ should suffer and on the third day rise from the dead, and that repentance and forgiveness of sins should be preached in his name to all nations, beginning from Jerusalem. You are witnesses of these things' (24.46–48).

This accords with the Lord's vision of the future when he said, 'Men will come from east and west, and from north and south, and sit at table in the kingdom of God' (13.29). Since men will come from the four corners of the earth it follows that people of *all* nations and races will be gathered into the kingdom of God's grace.

THE SAVIOUR'S PERFECT HUMANITY

Another aspect of Jesus which Luke portrays is his perfect humanity. This is an aspect which would have made a special appeal to the Greeks, for the perfecting of human personality was the ideal towards which they worked. Their gods were made in the likeness of men.

For this reason Luke is at pains to depict the manhood of Jesus as something unique yet utterly real. His Gospel is in a special sense the Gospel of the Son of Man—using that title in its simplest and most elementary sense. Jesus is not only truly and fully man; he is the pattern man, man as God intended him to be.

Birth and boyhood

This human aspect of the picture is seen at the beginning in Luke's matchless account of the nativity. It is a story which brings Jesus very near to us all, for he entered the world in the same way as we do, 'born of a woman'. While he was miraculously conceived in the womb, he was not miraculously born. His birth was as natural as that of any child. It was only the circumstances that were different. And it is Luke who depicts those circumstances: the over-crowded inn at Bethlehem, the birth in the stable at night, the infant laid in a manger (2.6, 7).

Again, to Luke we owe our only glimpse of the *boyhood* of Jesus when at twelve years of age he accompanied his parents to Jerusalem for the passover feast (2.41–52). The picture we get of him in the temple learning from the Jewish rabbis is an absorbing one. 'Jesus disputing with the doctors', some have called it. But the title is not a happy one. Jesus is learning in the same way as any boy of twelve athirst for knowledge would do when presented with the opportunity: by listening, by asking questions, by answering his teachers. Afterwards he returns with his parents to Nazareth, obediently taking his place in the family circle—and doubtless still learning in the synagogue and the home.

Against this background the evangelist speaks of his development, first from childhood to boyhood:

> The child grew and became strong, filled with wisdom; and the favour of God was upon him (2.40).

Next, from boyhood to manhood:

> Jesus increased in wisdom and in stature, and in favour with God and man (2.52).

In both cases his intellectual and spiritual growth is seen to be as real as his physical. At each stage of his life he is a complete human being.

Nothing more is related about Jesus until his baptism when he is anointed with the Holy Spirit (3.22). Then, as perfect and complete man, indwelt by the Spirit of God, he enters upon his life's work (see 4.1, 14, 18). Luke adds another human touch by saying that 'Jesus, when he began his ministry, was about thirty years of age' (3.23).

Jesus and prayer
Again and again in the course of that ministry the evangelist gives us insights into the Lord's humanity.

(i) Take for example his life of *prayer*. Prayer is a

very human instinct, signifying man's dependence on God. In his teaching Jesus had much to say on the subject, and here in this Gospel three of his parables about prayer are preserved:

the friend at midnight (11.5–8);
the unjust judge (18.1–8);
the Pharisee and the tax collector (18.9–14).

But more impressive than his teaching was Jesus' personal example in this matter. He himself was a man of prayer. Though he was the Son of God, yet as man he prayed to his Father in heaven. He gave himself specially to prayer before and during the great crises of his life. Luke records a number of such occasions:

at his baptism in the Jordan (3.21);
before choosing his twelve apostles (6.12);
before challenging the twelve regarding his messiahship (9.18);
at the transfiguration (9.29);
when teaching his disciples to pray (11.1);
on the cross for his murderers (23.34), and finally for himself in commitment to the Father (23.46).

(ii) Again, as man Jesus showed keen interest in *people* and kept company with all types—from the well-to-do religious Pharisees to the despised and detested tax collectors. On three occasions, Luke tells us, he accepted an invitation to dine in the house of a Pharisee (7.36; 11.37; 14.1). But he also mixed freely with those who were branded as 'sinners' and was equally ready to sit down to table with *them*, much to the disgust of the religious folk (15.1, 2; 19.5–7). Jesus was literally at home with all sorts and conditions of people. And who can forget the memorable scene when the sisters Martha and Mary entertained him in their home at Bethany? While the practical-minded Martha fussed around preparing an elaborate meal, her sister chose the 'better part' and sat quietly at the master's feet to listen to his teaching (10.38–42).

Women

(iii) *Women* play a specially prominent part in Luke's story. In the early chapters we meet with Elizabeth the wife of Zechariah and mother of John the Baptist; with Mary of Nazareth, the mother of our Lord; with Anna the prophetess in the temple. Later reference is made to the devoted band of women who ministered to Jesus and his disciples as they travelled through the towns and villages (8.1–3).

Luke delights to record the Lord's human compassion for the women he encountered in their hour of need. For example:

> the widow of Nain, to whom he gave back her only son from the dead (7.11–7);
> Mary Magdalene and other women whom he had delivered from their infirmities (8.2, 3);
> the woman who, bent double by her deformity, was 'made straight' at his word (13.11–13);
> the 'daughters of Jerusalem' who wept for him as he trod the road to Calvary (23.27, 28).

Luke's Gospel is rightly called the Gospel of womanhood. Both by his attitude and his teaching Jesus changed the position of women in society. It was a revolutionary change. He gave to woman a new status, a new dignity, a new freedom. He placed her on the same level as men. The Church as well as the world has been all too slow to catch up with his teaching.

52

Social concern

Yet another mark of the Lord's humanity may be noted. Luke shows him as a man with a *social concern*. He cared deeply for the poor; and there was a lot of poverty in Israel in his day owing to the taxes the Jews had to pay to the Romans in addition to their religious dues.

At the outset Jesus declared that he had come to preach good news to the poor (4.18; see also 7.22). In his sermon on the plain, as it has been called (6.17–49), he began with the words, 'Blessed are you poor, for yours is the kingdom of God.' In his parable of the great banquet—the banquet representing the kingdom of God—it is the well-to-do people who make excuses and refuse the invitation; it is the poor and needy and handicapped who are gathered in to enjoy the feast (14.16–24). And the Lord applied this to his hearers when he said:

> 'When you give a feast, invite the poor, the maimed, the lame, the blind, and you will be blessed, because they cannot repay you. You will be repaid at the resurrection of the just' (14.13, 14).

Jesus warns us against the peril of a materialistic attitude to life which loses sight of spiritual values:

> 'Take heed, and beware of all covetousness; for a man's life does not consist in the abundance of his possessions' (12.15).

He went on to illustrate the point by the parable of the rich fool—the story of a wealthy farmer whose barns were full but whose soul was empty. 'So is he who lays up treasure for himself, and is not rich towards God,' is Jesus' verdict.

Consider also the parable about the rich man (Dives) and the beggar Lazarus (16.19–31). Here

Jesus indicates the eternal consequences of the selfish misuse of money in this life. The rich man is condemned not because of his wealth but because of his callous indifference to human suffering when it was in his power to help. And in the end, in the future life, the roles of the two men are reversed. It is Lazarus who enjoys the blissful company of Abraham in the heavenly kingdom and Dives who becomes the beggar (v. 24).

Plainly Jesus as Luke portrays him is someone not remote from ourselves but as human as we are, 'the man Christ Jesus' (1 Timothy 2.5). He moves across the pages of the story in the nobility and dignity, grace and tenderness, of his manhood. He shared our life. He knew our sufferings. He had a deep insight into human nature and human need. He was made like his brethren in all things, sin only apart.

THE SAVIOUR OF THE LOST

Luke's story is, *par excellence*, the Gospel of the grace of God: his free, unmerited, unlimited love reaching down to the lowest and the least. Not without good reason it has been called the Gospel of the underdog. Jesus is seen as 'the friend of tax collectors and sinners' (7.34); and though the words were spoken in scorn and derision, they were true. If we were looking for a key phrase which sums up the whole Gospel we should find it in Jesus' own words: 'The Son of Man came to seek and to save the lost' (19.10). All words of one syllable—yet how much they say! In essence they set forth the programme and purpose of the Lord's ministry in this world.

The love of God
The love of God shines out all through Luke's record.

His is at once the most catholic and the most evangelical of the Gospels. Its catholicity is seen in its universal outlook, to which we have already drawn attention, proclaiming as it does the boundless *breadth* of God's love. Its evangelical character is seen in its gratuitous offer of salvation to the most fallen of mankind, thus magnifying the fathomless *depth* of God's love. Luke makes plain that the good news of salvation is for sinners only. There is no place in the kingdom of God for the self-righteous, the self-sufficient, the self-satisfied. He scatters the proud and exalts the humble; he satisfies the hungry and sends the rich empty away (1.51–53).

Illustrations of this abound in the Gospel. A good starting point would be the two opening verses of chapter 15.

> Now the tax collectors and sinners were all drawing near to hear him. And the Pharisees and the scribes murmured, saying, 'This man receives sinners and eats with them.'

Two contrasting groups are seen gathering round the Lord. On the one hand are the 'sinners', representing the outcasts and scum of society. Prominent among them are the contemptible tax collectors, notorious for their graft and hated for their collaboration with the Roman occupiers of Israel. On the other hand are the Pharisees and scribes, representing the establishment—the ultra-religious and respectable people of the day. They are scandalized at the sort of company Jesus is keeping. 'This fellow', they said, 'welcomes sinners and eats with them.' That Jesus should have any dealings at all with such people was bad enough. That he should actually sit at the same table with them was inexcusable.

Jesus answered their criticism by telling the three

parables which fill up the rest of the chapter. They are all stories of the lost: a lost sheep, a lost coin, and a lost son. These are the 'sinners'. It is noteworthy that Jesus does not deny that men are sinners or that they are lost—that is, lost to God, alienated from him because of their sin. But at the same time he insists that God's attitude to the lost is the exact opposite to that of the snobbish Pharisees. God loves the lost. He seeks the lost. They are of value to him—every single one of them. And when the lost are found, he rejoices in their recovery and all heaven shares his joy.

Here in passing we may note that *joy* is one of the leading features of this Gospel. And it is the Gospel of joy because it is the Gospel of salvation. Again and again in its pages we read about people 'glorifying God' for what Jesus had done for them (for examples, see 5.25; 7.16; 13.13; 17.15; 18.43).

Another parable which reveals God's love for the sinner is that about the Pharisee and tax collector who went to the temple to pray (18.9–14). Yet how differently they prayed. The Pharisee, full of his own righteousness, boasted of his strict moral and religious life and thanked God he was so much better than the rest of men. The tax collector, on the other hand, had nothing to boast about, no merit of his own to plead. He knew he was a sinner and could only cry to God for mercy. And he obtained mercy, for Jesus said (v. 14 NEB):

> 'It was this man, I tell you, and not the other, who went home acquitted of his sins. For everyone who exalts himself will be humbled; and whoever humbles himself will be exalted.'

The prostitute
We turn from the parables and look at three stories

56

which portray Jesus as the saviour of the lost. They are stories of his encounters with a prostitute, a tax collector and a robber.

The first is related in 7.36–50. The scene is the house of a Pharisee called Simon who invited Jesus to dine with him. During the meal a woman of the city who had been notorious for her immoral life knelt behind Jesus as he reclined at table and anointed his feet, kissing them and anointing them with her hair. Evidently on some previous occasion she had met with the Lord, confessed her sin, and received forgiveness. Now as a penitent sinner she returns to give thanks to him for all he had done for her. Her tears, her kisses, her anointing of his feet, were the expression of her deep gratitude and devotion.

Simon the Pharisee, not knowing the woman's story and having little sense of God's grace in his own life, failed to understand what was happening and was shocked. The woman was a sinner! How could Jesus allow her to touch him? But Jesus understood, and by telling a simple parable about two debtors he explained the woman's actions. She 'loved much' because she had been forgiven much (v. 47). Her love was not the cause but the consequence of her forgiveness. It was her *faith* that saved her, as Jesus assured her when he sent her away in peace (v. 50).

The tax collector
The next story is about Zacchaeus, the wealthy tax collector (19.1–10). He was, it seems, the superintendent of taxes at Jericho and may well have been the richest man in the town. He was almost certainly the most detested. He was doubtless ostracized by all decent people on account of his job—a desperately lonely man.

He sought to see Jesus, it is said. But the significant thing is that Jesus was actually seeking *him*, and when he found him hiding up a tree he pressed upon him an urgent invitation: 'Zacchaeus, today I must stay at your house!'

It was a remarkable gesture of friendship on the part of Jesus. When he entered Zacchaeus's house the crowd strongly disapproved, such was the tax collector's unsavoury reputation (v. 7). We are not told what passed between him and Jesus in the house, but we know the outcome. Zacchaeus was converted! And he demonstrated the fact by what he did. Renouncing his old life he immediately handed over half his fortune to the poor and made full restitution to those he had wronged. No wonder Jesus said, 'Salvation has come to this house today!'

The cross

The third story is that of the penitent thief and brings us to the cross (23.39–43).

> One of the criminals who were hanged railed at Jesus, saying, 'Are you not the Christ? Save yourself and us!' But the other rebuked him, saying, 'Do you not fear God, since you are under the same sentence of condemnation? And we indeed justly; for we are receiving the due reward of our deeds; but this man has done nothing wrong.' And he said, 'Jesus, remember me when you come in your kingly power.' And he said to him, 'Truly, I say to you, today you will be with me in Paradise.'

The story speaks for itself and calls for little comment. Here indeed, in Bunyan's words, is grace abounding to a chief of sinners: a man who was lost and acknowledged it. Hence his prayer, 'Jesus, remember me', received an immediate answer, for Jesus had come to seek and to save the lost. And this thief, as it has been said, was a total loss until he found Jesus—and Jesus found him—at Calvary.

The incident lies at the heart of Luke's record of the crucifixion and has a deep significance. It interprets to us the purpose and meaning of the cross.

As the Saviour of the lost Jesus identified himself with sinners—in his death as in his life. When he died he was 'reckoned with transgressors', as the prophet had foretold (Isaiah 53.12; see Luke 22.37). But more. He not only suffered *with* sinners; he also suffered *for* them, as the prophet had likewise written in the same context: 'he bore the sin of many'. It was by his sin-bearing that Jesus achieved the redemption of mankind, and in doing so he opened the kingdom of heaven to all who believe in him—including the dying robber.

The resurrection

Luke's account of the resurrection in the final chapter stresses the fact of the empty tomb. But that in itself was not enough to convince the disciples that Jesus had risen from the dead. It was his *appearances* to them at different times and in different ways that dispelled their doubts and kindled faith in him as the living Saviour.

Dominating the chapter is the superbly told story of the walk to Emmaus (24.13–35). It describes the transforming effect of the resurrection on two quite ordinary disciples. They set out from Jerusalem that first Easter day with perplexed minds and despondent hearts. They were sad, disillusioned, without hope. But when unrecognized 'Jesus himself drew near and went with them', everything was changed. He walked

59

with them and talked with them, explaining so many things in the Bible they had never understood; and soon their hearts were aglow. It is a picture of what happens when the Jesus of history becomes the Christ of experience. In successive scenes he is set before us as the companion of life's daily journey, the interpreter of the scriptures, the guest in the home, the president at the sacramental meal.

The chapter ends with a brief record of the Lord's ascension, his last visible appearance to this disciples.

> He lead them out as far as Bethany, and lifting up his hands he blessed them. While he blessed them, he parted from them. And they returned to Jerusalem with great joy, and were continually in the temple blessing God.

So the Gospel ends, as it began, in the temple, and on a note of joy and praise.

4
John
The Incarnate Son

'LAST of all,' wrote Clement of Alexandria about the year 200, 'John, when he saw that the outward (bodily) facts had been set forth in the earlier Gospels, being urged by his friends and inspired by the Spirit, composed a spiritual Gospel.'

No better description than this has been given of the distinctive character of the fourth Gospel. It is essentially a *spiritual* Gospel. As such it not only supplements the other three Gospels. It completes the New Testament portrait of Jesus by setting forth his unique relation to God the Father.

In many respects John's Gospel stands alone. The three earlier ones belong together and are therefore called the Synoptic Gospels, because they adopt a common viewpoint in relating the story of Jesus' life and work. They use much the same language, adhere to much the same order, cover much the same ground. The fourth Gospel is different. In its record of the Lord's ministry (especially his Judaean ministry) his teaching, his miraculous works, his death and resurrection, it shows itself to be independent of the others. It goes deeper than they do. It is more than an historical record. It discloses the meaning of the things Jesus said and did. It penetrates into his heart and mind. It is indeed a spiritual Gospel.

61

The purpose

Luke, as we saw, stated his purpose in writing his Gospel at the very outset. John does so at the end of his work. In chapter 20.30, 31 (the original conclusion of the book, chapter 21 being an appendix) he writes:

> Now Jesus did many other signs in the presence of the disciples, which are not written in this book; but these are written that you may believe that Jesus is the Christ, the Son of God, and that believing you may have life in his name.

This statement is the key to the understanding of the Gospel. Its message can be summed up in a short sentence: *life through believing in the Son of God*. Every word here is important.

(i) The evangelist makes it clear that his aim is to portray Jesus in a particular light: not simply as the *Christ*, the promised Messiah of Israel, but as one who is in a unique sense the *Son of God*. This is the characteristic title given to him in the Gospel. In 138 verses he is spoken of as the 'Son' in relation to the Father.

(ii) *Eternal life* is another key phrase. The verb 'to live' and the noun 'life' occur well over fifty times. And this eternal life—life of a divine, spiritual quality as distinct from human, physical existence—is God's gift to all who will receive it.

(iii) It is received by *faith* in Christ—a third key word. There are nearly a hundred references to faith or believing, and in every instance the word means personal trust, not simply adherence to a creed.

John makes clear that in writing his Gospel he has not attempted a complete record. Jesus did many other things than those he has related. He has carefully selected the material which would further

his purpose and enable his readers to see in Jesus the
person of the Son of God, so that through faith in him
they might possess eternal life.

THE SON OF GOD MADE FLESH

We have been looking at the ending of the Gospel. We
must come back to its beginning. The prologue
which forms the first eighteen verses is one of the
most important and profound passages in the whole
Bible. Its significance lies in the way in which it
introduces us to the person of Christ and in doing so
epitomizes the story which the evangelist is about to
unfold. We will look at it in the words of the New
English Bible.

> When all things began, the Word already was.
> The Word dwelt with God, and what God was,
> the Word was. The Word, then, was with God at
> the beginning, and through him all things came
> to be; no single thing was created without him.
> All that came to be was alive with his life, and
> that life was the light of men. The light shines in
> the dark, and the darkness has never mastered it.

Jesus the Word of God

What immediately arrests our attention in these first
five verses is the title given to Jesus: the 'Word'
(*Logos*) of God. It is a title which conveys the idea of
revelation. 'Logos means not only the spoken word,
but the thought expressed by the spoken word; it is
the spoken word as expressive of thought'
(A. Plummer). Just as word utters thought, so does
Christ utter God. He is the Word of God made visible
as well as audible. God has spoken to us in the person
of his Son (Hebrews 1.1, 2).

The verses quoted reveal who Jesus is in three ways.

(i) First, in relation to *God*. We learn of his pre-existence: 'When all things began, the Word already was'—i.e. before the world came into being. We learn of his personality: 'The Word dwelt with God', distinct from him yet in perfect communion with him. We learn of his divinity: 'What God was, the Word was'—i.e. the essential nature of God was his.

(ii) Next, in relation to the *created order*. The Word was the agent of creation: 'through him all things came to be; no single thing was created without him'. He is also the source of life, for 'all that came to be was alive with his life'.

(iii) Third, in relation to *humanity*. The Word not only gives life to all living creatures; he is 'the *light* of men'. Light here means moral and spiritual illumination. It is this that distinguishes mankind from the rest of the animal creation.

Christ's coming to men
All this is deeply theological. Now (vv. 6–9) the prologue continues on a different level, the historical level. It deals with the entrance of Christ the light-giver into the world's spiritual darkness. John the Baptist had prepared the way for this momentous event by bearing witness to the light—that is, to Christ; for he, the true light, was 'even then coming into the world' (v. 9).

What happened when he came? Verses 10–13 supply the answer:

> He was in the world; but the world, though it owed its being to him, did not recognize him. He entered his own realm, and his own would not receive him. But to all who did receive him, to

those who have yielded him their allegiance, he gave the right to become children of God, not born of any human stock, or by the fleshly desire of a human father, but the offspring of God himself.

Here is John's Gospel in brief. When Christ entered his own realm (Israel), his own people (the Jews) would not receive him. They did not believe his claim to be the Son of God. But there were some who did believe and who by receiving him became God's children by means of a new and spiritual birth.

Throughout the Gospel, as we shall see, those to whom Christ came reacted to him in one or other of these ways. At the outset of his story the evangelist is hinting at the conflict that was to ensue between the unbelief of the Jews who rejected him and the faith of the disciples who gave him their allegiance.

The Word made flesh
We are now prepared for the crowning statement in verse 14:

> So the Word became flesh; he came to dwell among us, and we saw his glory, such glory as befits the Father's only Son, full of grace and truth.

'*The Word became flesh*'. John's Gospel is supremely the Gospel of the incarnation. It is this truth that lies at the heart of the Christian religion. The Word who *was* God from all eternity and therefore partaker of the devine nature, *became* flesh, assuming a true human nature like our own.

Christ is the God-Man, one person, at once wholly divine and wholly human. As such he 'dwelt among us' (literally 'tabernacled' among us); and just as

God's glory had filled the tabernacle of old (Exod. 40.34), so now the same glory was manifested in his incarnate Son, 'full of grace and truth'. Those who saw him in his earthly life could bear witness to this.

The prologue ends with the words, 'No one has ever seen God; but God's only Son, he who is nearest to the Father's heart, he has made him known.' Later in the Gospel Jesus makes the same claim for himself (14.9). He is 'the image of the invisible God' (Col. 1.15). Hence the story of Jesus in this Gospel is the truth about God. 'It is the word "God" translated into human terms and spelt out in human words and acts. All that mortal men can take in about the nature of the unseen God is ours in Jesus Christ' (A. M. Hunter, *Cambridge Bible Commentary*, *Gospel according to St John*, CUP, 1965, p. 21).

The main emphasis in this Gospel is on the deity of Christ. At the time it was written—near the end of the first century—there were those in the Church who questioned this truth. They taught that while Jesus was a divine being, *like* God, he was not truly one with God. This was the view that later developed into the Arian heresy. At the same time there were others who, while holding fast to the Godhead of Jesus, had doubts about the reality of his manhood. These were the Gnostics who taught that he was not truly and fully human: he only *appeared* to be such.

The Gospel of John has the answer to both these errors. It affirms that Jesus is the eternal Word who nevertheless became *flesh*; and it makes clear that the flesh of Jesus was real flesh, with all its limitations and weaknesses. There are a number of instances which confirm and illustrate the Lord's humanity.

He was guest at a wedding feast in Cana (2.1–11).

He was tired and rested at Jacob's well (4.6).

He wept at the grave of Lazarus (11.35).

He washed his disciples' feet at the last supper
(13.3–5).

He uttered the cry 'I thirst' on the cross (19.28).

Again, after he had died, one of the soldiers pierced his side with a lance, 'and at once there flowed out blood and water' (19.34). Whatever symbolism may be read into this (cf. 1 John 5.6–8), there is no doubt that Jesus' death was real; his body was no mere semblance.

The person of Jesus as John portrays him is the Word-made-flesh: one with God as the eternal Son and one with us as a man of flesh and blood.

THE SON MANIFESTED TO THE WORLD

After the prologue the evangelist has something further to say about the witness of John the Baptist (1.19–34). He relates how, through his witness, the first disciples were drawn to Jesus, including the apostles John, Andrew and Peter (1.35–51).

At this point we may note that the Gospel has much to say about the witness borne to Jesus in the course of his ministry. In fact *witness* is one of the evangelist's dominant themes: the word occurs nearly fifty times. Apart from the witness of the Baptist there is a series of other testimonies to the claims of the Son of God:

the witness of the Samaritan woman (4.39);
the witness of the works of Jesus (5.36);
the witness of the Father (5.37);
the witness of the scriptures (5.39);
the witness of the Holy Spirit (15.26);
the witness of the disciples (15.27);
the witness of the Gospel writer (19.35).

The record of the Lord's public ministry—his manifestation to the world, more especially to Israel—begins at chapter 2 and continues to the end of chapter 12. We will take note of some of its special features.

The seven signs

Among these features are the seven miracles of Jesus recorded in the main body of the Gospel, excluding chapter 21. The evangelist does not call them miracles—i.e. simply works of supernatural power—but *signs*. Thus at the end of the first of them he writes: 'This, the first of his signs, did Jesus at Cana in Galilee, and manifested his glory' (2.11). The miracles are signs because they have an inner meaning. They signify some aspect of divine truth and display the 'glory' or essential nature of the incarnate Son.

(i) The turning of water into wine at Cana (2.1–11) was an act of transformation, symbolizing in dramatic form the work which the Son of God came on earth to do. He came to change the old order of the law into the new order of grace. Judaism is water; Christianity is wine. By his regenerating power Christ transfigures and enriches the whole life of man.

(ii) The healing of the royal officer's son (4.46–54) illustrates the nature and necessity of *faith* in salvation. It was his faith that brought the man to Jesus. He believed the Lord could heal his son—if only he were present on the spot. Hence his urgent entreaty, 'Sir, come down before my child dies.' But Jesus did not go with him. Instead he gave the man a promise: 'Go, your son will live.' The man took Jesus at his word, trusted his promise, and his faith was rewarded.

(iii) The cure of the man who had been a cripple for thirty-eight years (5.2–9) shows Christ to be the restorer of lost powers. In the words of William Temple, 'Our fellowship with Christ not only hallows and intensifies all the powers that we have when we first meet with him. He restores those which are atrophied by neglect or abuse' (*Readings in St John's Gospel*, Macmillan, 1945, p. 107).

(iv) The feeding of the five thousand (6.4–13)—the only miracle related by all four evangelists—signifies Christ to be the bread of life which alone can satisfy the hunger of the human heart. The discourse which follows later in the chapter (vv. 25–51) amplifies this truth and insists that it is by faith that the individual appropriates Christ, the true bread from heaven.

(v) The sign of Jesus walking on the water and coming to the aid of his disciples when caught in a storm at sea (6.16–21) demonstrates a further truth. Christ is the companion and succourer of his people in the storms of life; and his presence not only brings them peace but guides them safely to their desired haven.

(vi) The granting of sight to the man born blind (9.1–7) reveals Christ as the giver of light. The story is an enacted parable of the spiritual illumination which issues from faith in Christ and enables the believer to say, 'Once I was blind, but now I see.'

(vii) The last and greatest of the signs is the raising of Lazarus from the dead (11.1–44). Christ is our life as well as our light. As this Gospel constantly stresses, his mission was to bring eternal life within reach of all. 'I came,' he declared, 'that they may have life, and have it abundantly' (10.10; see also 5.21).

Dialogues and discourses
The Son of God manifested himself to the world in word as well as in deed. Another outstanding feature of this Gospel is its account of the dialogues Jesus had with certain people and his public discourses.

The first of the dialogues (3.1–15) was with Nicodemus: a representative of Judaism at its best. For Nicodemus was a devout Jew, a highly moral man, a revered teacher of the law. He comes to Jesus secretly by night as one who is seeking further religious knowledge. Jesus tells him that his basic need is not light but *life*; not religion but regeneration (vv. 3, 6):

> Truly, truly I say to you, unless one is born anew, he cannot see the kingdom of God . . . That which is born of the flesh is flesh and that which is born of the Spirit is spirit.

Life moves on two levels, flesh and spirit, the natural and the supernatural. To be born of the flesh is to have physical life—that, and nothing more. Spiritual life needs spiritual birth, and this is the work of the Holy Spirit the life-giver.

In the next chapter Jesus has a conversation with a very different sort of person. The woman he met at Jacob's well was not only a Samaritan—i.e. of alien race—but a woman of disreputable moral character. She had come to draw water. He offered her 'living (life-giving) water' which would satisfy her thirsting soul for ever. When the conversation was becoming too personal for her liking she created a diversion by asking, Which is the true place to worship God—the Jewish temple in Jerusalem or the Samaritan one on Mount Gerizim? Jesus told her that true worship is not a question of *where* but of *how*. 'God is spirit,' he declared, independent of time and space, and therefore worship must be spiritual, inward, sincere (vv. 23, 24).

John records at length in chapters 7 and 8 a dialogue Jesus had with the Jewish authorities in Jerusalem during the feast of Tabernacles. They challenged him as to his person and origin. 'Who are you? Where do you come from?' Jesus answered their questions in words like these:

> I have not come of my own accord; he who sent me is true, and him you do not know. I know him, for I come from him, and he sent me (7.28, 29).

> I do nothing on my own authority but speak thus as the Father taught me. And he who sent me is with me; he has not left me alone, for I always do what is pleasing to him (8.28, 29).

> If God were your Father, you would love me, for I proceeded and came forth from God (8.42).

The Jews rejected Jesus' claims and attempted to stone him as a blasphemer (8.59).

The claims of Jesus

The claims of Jesus are set forth most clearly in his public discourses. One of these is in chapter 5.19–47, following his healing of the cripple on the sabbath (vv. 1–9). The Jews denounced him as a sabbath-breaker. He answered them by defining his unique relation to the Father as the judge of mankind and the life-giver. These are manifestly divine offices; but they belong to Jesus in view of the perfect harmony between the Father and the Son. Thus it is that he possesses both the authority to judge men in the last day and the power to give them life in the present. Accordingly he demands that all men should honour the Son even as they honour the Father (v. 23). The supernatural claims of Jesus in this whole passage are the plainest vindication of his Godhead.

The discourse on the bread of life which follows the feeding of the five thousand (6.25–58) is too well known to call for comment. It is best summed up in the Lord's own words (v. 51 NEB):

> I am that living bread which has come down from heaven; if anyone eats this bread he shall live for ever. Moreover, the bread which I will give him is my own flesh; I give it for the life of the world.

The connection between this discourse, with its reference to eating Christ's flesh and drinking his blood, and the sacrament of the Lord's Supper is inescapable. The fourth Gospel does not record the institution of the Eucharist but in these words of Jesus its spiritual value is explained. In the sacrament we personally assimilate by faith the benefits of the Lord's passion and make them our own; and to be thus united with him is to partake of the divine, eternal life he bestows.

Another well known discourse is in chapter 10—the good shepherd chapter as it is often called. Here the Lord declares himself to be not only the shepherd of the flock, who voluntarily lays down his life for the sheep (vv. 11–15), but also the door, the only door, into the sheepfold. 'When he brings us to the Father,' wrote Chrysostom, 'he calls himself a door; when he takes care of us, he calls himself a shepherd.' His words are in part an indictment of the Jewish authorities as false and faithless shepherds, in accordance with Ezekiel 34.

Much of the Lord's teaching in this Gospel is summed up in his memorable 'I am' sayings, the seven parables of the Lord's person, as William Temple called them. They can be seen as corresponding to the seven signs.

> 'I am the bread of life; he who comes to me shall not hunger' (6.35).

'I am the light of the world; he who follows me will not walk in darkness, but will have the light of life' (8.12).

'I am the door of the sheep . . . if anyone enters by me, he will be saved' (10.7, 9).

'I am the good shepherd. The good shepherd lays down his life for the sheep' (10.11).

'I am the resurrection and the life; he who believes in me, though he die, yet shall he live, and whoever lives and believes in me shall never die' (11.25).

'I am the way, and the truth, and the life; no one comes to the Father, but by me' (14.6).

'I am the true vine, . . . you are the branches. He who abides in me, and I in him, he it is that bears much fruit' (15.1, 5).

Singly and as a body these words bear witness to the uniqueness of Christ. They testify to his divine person and saving mission; they assert who he is and what he does for those who appropriate him by faith.

Faith and unbelief

Such claims consistently brought Jesus into conflict with the Jewish authorities, who as consistently rejected his claims and sought to silence him. At the same time his words and works increased and strengthened the faith of the disciples. Accordingly Bishop Westcott asserted that the plan of the Gospel is 'to express as briefly as possible the parallel development of faith and unbelief through the historical presence of Christ'; and he analysed the contents of the Gospel—apart from the prologue (1.1–18) and epilogue (ch. 21)—as follows.

- (i) The revelation of the Messiah: beginnings of faith and unbelief (1.19–6.71).
- (ii) The great conflict: development of unbelief among the Jews (chs. 7–12).
- (iii) The fuller revelation: development of faith among the disciples (chs. 13–17).
- (iv) The passion: climax of unbelief among the Jews (chs. 18–19).
- (v) The empty tomb: climax of faith among the disciples (ch. 20).

The conclusion of the Lord's public ministry is recorded in chapter 12. At this early point we reach the story of the triumphal entry into Jerusalem (vv. 12–19), viz. the beginning of the last great week. At the end of the chapter the evangelist provides an epilogue to the public ministry (vv. 37–50). He quotes from Isaiah 53 to show that the rejection of the Messiah had been foretold in the scriptures; and finally he records some of the Lord's own words, summing up his mission as the one sent by the Father to bring the light of salvation to the world.

THE REVELATION OF THE SON TO THE DISCIPLES

The way is now prepared for the narrative of the passion. But before that, beginning at chapter 13 and continuing to the end of chapter 17, we have the Lord's 'fuller revelation' of himself to the disciples in the privacy of the upper room at the last supper.

It is the night before the crucifixion. Unlike the other evangelists—as we have already noted—John does not give an account of the institution of the Eucharist. His readers were already familiar with that. Instead, he tells of Jesus' action in washing the disciples' feet (13.2–17). This in itself is doubtless to be regarded as having a sacramental value, illustrating the cleansing power of his approaching sacrifice. Symbolically he lays aside his garments (his glory) and takes the form of a servant, that he might stoop yet further to the death of the cross (Phil. 2.5–8).

With the departure of Judas the traitor (vv. 21–30) the Lord is now able to speak freely to his faithful followers. He wishes to prepare them for what lies ahead: his imminent separation from them, his return to the Father, and their future mission in the world. The parting is at hand; but before he leaves them he has some final things to say to them by way of command, promise and warning.

Final injunctions
In chapter 13.33–35 he speaks to them about their relationship one with another as his disciples. 'A new commandment I give to you, that you love one another; even as I have loved you, that you also love one another.' The commandment is *new* because it is to be operative within the new society of the Church. New also because it is based on a new standard of love—nothing less than Christ's own self-sacrificing love for them. Such love is to be the distinguishing mark of Christian discipleship in the eyes of the world.

He tells them not to be troubled in heart because he is leaving them, for he is going to the Father (14.1 ff.). He assures them that in his Father's house there is room for all and that he is going there on purpose to prepare a place for them. Thomas wants to know the way to God. 'I am the way,' Jesus tells him; 'no one comes to the Father, but by me.' Then Philip has a request: 'Lord, show us the Father, and we shall be satisfied.' His answer is simple. 'Do you not know *me*, Philip? He who has seen me has seen the Father.'

The all-important thing for the disciples during Jesus' physical absence is to keep in spiritual contact with him. He illustrates this by the allegory of the vine in chapter 15.1–17. The vine branches bear fruit only as long as they are in close and vital union with the vine. So the disciples must remain in unbroken union with Christ. Their fruitfulness depends wholly on this. Severed from him they can do nothing.

The gift of the Spirit
A notable feature of this discourse is the Lord's teaching about the gift of the Holy Spirit (see 14.15–26; 15.26–27; 16.7–15). Consider his promise in chapter 14.15–18:

> If you love me, you will keep my commandments. And I will pray the Father, and he will give you another counsellor (advocate), to be with you for ever, even the Spirit of truth, whom the world cannot receive . . . I will not leave you desolate (orphans); I will come to you.

Christ here closely identifies the promised Spirit with himself. It is important to remember this. The Holy Spirit is the Spirit of Christ, Christ in us, Christ's other self. For the Spirit was given at Pentecost not to compensate for Christ's absence but to ensure Christ's presence. Thus the believer is 'in Christ' and Christ is in the believer.

It is in the power of his Spirit that the Lord sends the disciples into the world to bear witness for him. He warns them that it is a hostile world into which they are going; it will treat them as it treated him (see 15.18–21). In chapter 16.1–5 he illustrates this point in relation to his immediate disciples. They must be ready to face persecution, excommunication and martyrdom for his sake. But his final words to them are full of encouragement: 'I have told you all this so that in me you may find peace. In the world you will have trouble. But courage! The victory is mine; I have overcome the world' (16.33 NEB).

The prayer of Jesus

When he had finished his teaching Jesus turned to prayer (chapter 17). It is commonly called the 'high priestly prayer', for here Jesus enters as it were the holy of holies. The Jewish high priest, on the solemn day of atonement, having made sacrifice for the nation's sin, passed through the temple veil to intercede with God for the whole congregation of Israel. So now Jesus, in the consciousness of his completed sacrifice (v. 4), prays to the Father: first for the disciples there gathered around him (vv. 6–19) and then for all who would later believe in him because of their witness (vv. 20–26).

His prayer for the Church of the then future—the Church of today—is deeply significant. He prayed for its visible unity, that as a living fellowship of the Spirit it might demonstrate God's saving love to the world. And his final petition (v. 24) was that the Church militant on earth might become the Church triumphant in heaven.

THE SON OF GOD GLORIFIED

Chapters 18–21 are the final section of the Gospel. They are concerned with the crucifixion and resurrection: the climax of unbelief among the Jews and the climax of faith among the disciples.

At this point the Gospel links up with the passion story in the other Gospels. But as we might expect, John relates the historical events from a distinctive point of view, independently of the others, and interprets their inner meaning. Westcott points out that in its account of the crucifixion the Gospel gives prominence to three matters: the voluntary nature of Christ's sufferings; the fulfilment of a divine plan in Christ's sufferings; and the majesty which shines through Christ's sufferings.

The glory of the cross

One matter demands our attention: the view of the cross in this Gospel as being Christ's *glory* rather than his shame. On three occasions Jesus had spoken of his approaching death in terms of his being 'glorified' (see 12.23, 24; 13.31; 17.1). The evangelist uses the expression in the same way in chapter 7.39 and chapter 12.16. In what sense is it to be understood?

The cross is the moment of Christ's supreme glory because by his self-sacrificing love he perfectly accomplished the Father's will, made atonement for the sin of the world, vanquished the power of death, and opened the kingdom of heaven to all who believe in him. This glorification includes the whole of his redemptive action: not only his death but also his resurrection and exaltation and the sending of the Holy Spirit. So William Temple writes: 'The Cross is the glory of God because self-sacrifice is the expression of love. That glory would be complete in itself even if it had no consequences. But in fact what is revealed in the Cross is not only the perfection of divine love, but its triumph' (*Readings in St John's Gospel*, Macmillan, 1945, p. 308).

The passion story proper begins with the arrest of Jesus in the garden of Gethsemane (18.1–11). The dramatic scene is dominated by the sense of the

Lord's majesty: his absolute mastery of the situation as, unarmed and apparently helpless, he confronts his foes. He exhibits the same majestic bearing at his trial when he is brought successively before the Jewish authorities (18.12–14 and 19–24) and the Roman governor (18.28–19.16).

John's account of the civil trial is by far the longest and most detailed version of this. Clearly Pilate is impressed by the dignity and demeanour of his prisoner and by what he has to say. Three times Jesus speaks to him about 'my kingdom', or better (as RSV) 'my kingship' (18.36); but he explains that his sovereignty is a spiritual one and belongs to a higher realm than earthly politics. Three times Pilate addresses the crowd and pronounces him innocent (18.39; 19.4, 6); but nothing he says will satisfy the frenzied mob. When offered the choice they prefer the gangster Barabbas to Jesus. The choice was symbolic: symbolic of the unbelieving world's attitude to Christ the king and its own distorted scale of values.

Pilate at last gives way. Handed over to be executed, Jesus is led to Golgotha and crucified between two criminals. 'On either side one and Jesus in the midst', says the evangelist, indicating the centrality of the cross. Among the bystanders looking on is Mary the mother of Jesus, whom he commits to the care of the beloved disciple. 'Woman, behold your son!' he says to her; and to John, 'Behold your mother!' Two other sayings of Jesus from the cross are peculiar to this Gospel (19.28–30): 'I thirst', indicative of Jesus' intense physical anguish, and 'It is finished!'—the victor's cry of achievement.

The body of Jesus is buried on the Friday evening in the garden tomb provided by Joseph of Arimathaea and there it rests on the Jewish sabbath (Saturday).

The risen Lord

At dawn on the Sunday morning—'the first day of the week', as the evangelist significantly calls it—the tomb is found by Jesus' disciples to be empty: empty, that is, except for the undisturbed grave clothes. The fact of the empty tomb is strongly emphasized and clearly attested (20.1–9).

But John's record of the resurrection, as we should expect, is not simply concerned with an historical happening. It is a revelation of spiritual truth. Three appearances of the risen Lord are related in chapter 20. They can be seen to represent the triumph of faith over personal sorrow, in the case of Mary Magdalene (vv. 10–18); over common fear, on the part of the disciples hiding behind locked doors (vv. 19–23); and over individual doubt, as seen in Thomas's refusal to believe without tangible proof (vv. 24–29).

With the story of Thomas we reach the climax of faith among the disciples.

> Eight days later his disciples were again in the house, and Thomas was with them. The doors were shut, but Jesus came and stood among them, and said, 'Peace be with you.' Then he said to Thomas, 'Put your finger here, and see my hands; and put out your hand, and place it in my side; do not be faithless, but believing.' Thomas answered him, 'My Lord and my God!' Jesus said to him, 'Have you believed because you have seen me? Blessed are those who have not seen and yet believe.'

By his confession Thomas the doubter rises to the loftiest view of the Lord given in any of the Gospels. Jesus accepts it and pronounces a blessing on all who share the same faith without the same evidence. So here at the end of the story we are back where we began: 'The Word (Jesus) was God.' As Professor A. M. Hunter remarks, the wheel of the Gospel has turned full circle. Its testimony to Jesus is meant to lead its readers to precisely this confession: *My Lord and my God!*

The final chapter (21), as we have noted, is not part of the Gospel proper, but forms an appendix. It records the appearance of the risen Lord to a group of disciples by the Sea of Galilee and his gracious dealings with Simon Peter and the beloved disciple. The story might have been extended even further, for as the writer of the postscript states:

> There is much else that Jesus did. If it were all to be recorded in detail, I suppose the whole world would not hold the books that would be written (21.25 NEB).

A pardonable hyperbole, this; 'for to tell the whole story of Jesus' love and power would exhaust the capacities of the universe' (William Temple, *Readings in St John's Gospel*, Macmillan, 1945, p. 412).

Epilogue
The One Lord

WE have looked in turn at the Gospel portraits and taken note of their distinctive features. But let us be clear that in looking at the four different portraits we have not been looking at four different persons. While the portraits are four, the person is one and the same. There are four Gospels and one Lord, four records with one purpose—that purpose being to impart to mankind the knowledge of Jesus Christ.

It is this that gives the Gospels their unique value and supreme importance. As W. E. Gladstone wrote: 'Christianity is Christ, and nearness to him and to his image is the end of all our efforts. Thus the Gospels, which continually present to us one pattern, have a kind of precedence among the books of Holy Scripture.'

Each of the Gospels, as we have seen, makes its own contribution to the total portrait of Jesus. We also noted at the outset that the evangelists, in selecting their materials, were guided by the needs and interests of the people for whom they wrote. Hence in reading them we find ourselves looking at the one Lord from four angles.

>In *Matthew* we see him in his messianic role as the promised *king*, fulfilling the Jewish scriptures.

>In *Mark* we see him in his ceaseless ministry as

the Lord's *servant*, obediently treading the appointed path of suffering and sacrifice.

In *Luke* we see him in the perfection of his manhood as the *saviour* of the world and friend of sinners.

In *John* we see him in his self-humiliation as the everlasting Son of the Father, made flesh for us.

All the evangelists point us directly to Jesus, but in doing so they reveal him in these varied aspects. We may adopt some words from the Old Testament prophets and hear Matthew saying 'Behold, your king' (Zech. 9.9); Mark 'Behold my servant' (Isa. 42.1); Luke 'Behold, the man' (Zech. 6.12); and John 'Behold your God' (Isa. 40.9).

That the Gospels possess such characteristic features has been acknowledged from the beginning. For example, as far back as the second century Christian writers discerned a likeness between the four books and the four 'living creatures' of Revelation 4.7—the lion, the ox, the man, and the eagle. These may be seen as symbolical of kingship (Matthew), service (Mark), humanity (Luke), and divinity (John). The figures may also be allocated in other ways.

This line of thought has continued to attract attention through the centuries. It is of course largely fanciful and probably makes little appeal today. Nevertheless it does indicate that the Church has always recognized the significance of the fourfold Gospel in presenting the fourfold portrait of the one Lord.

This portrait is presented to us not simply to win our admiration but to challenge our faith. The one Lord claims our allegiance. For the Gospels are more than just historical documents, recording certain things that happened. They are essentially religious documents, providing also an interpretation of those happenings.

This is particularly true as we have seen in the case of the Gospel of John. But it applies to the others as well. And it is for this reason that the books all bear the title of *gospel*—that is, good news. The writers are not only chroniclers of facts. They are gospellers, evangelists, preachers, and the good news they publish to the world has as its creative centre the person of Jesus Christ our Lord.

Plainly we owe them an incalculable debt for their fourfold portrait. Professor F. F. Bruce admirably sums it up in the following words: 'The four evangelists, writing from their different points of view, concur in presenting us with a comprehensive, sufficient and heart-compelling portrayal of Jesus as Messiah of Israel and Saviour of the world, Servant of the Lord and Friend of sinners, Son of God and Son of Man' (*A New Testament Commentary*, ed. H. H. Howley, Pickering & Inglis, 1969, p. 101).

To that we may add one further quotation:

'Take the Scriptures, read them, and in the measure that the Father grants it you will meet the Son. The countenance of our Lord, turned towards you personally, cannot be depicted to you by another: you must see it for yourself. And you must allow no one to turn you aside from doing so; for in your thus meeting your Lord personally lies the greatest boon that can be granted you' (Romano Guardini).